W9-AUG-927

1 MAY '67 LD   **DATE DUE**

NOV 20 1967

MAR 29 1972

WHAT
IN THE WORLD?

WHAT
IN THE
WORLD
?

by

COLIN W. WILLIAMS

EXECUTIVE DIRECTOR OF THE
CENTRAL DEPARTMENT OF EVANGELISM
NATIONAL COUNCIL OF THE CHURCHES OF CHRIST IN THE U.S.A.
CHAIRMAN OF THE DEPARTMENT ON STUDIES IN EVANGELISM
WORLD COUNCIL OF CHURCHES

Copyright © 1964
by Colin W. Williams
2d Printing, May 1965
3d Printing, September 1965

This book is not an official document of the National Council of the Churches of Christ in the United States of America. It is prepared for use in study groups exploring changing forms of the Church's witness as a part of the long range study of "The Missionary Structure of the Congregation" authorized by the World Council of Churches at its Third Assembly at New Delhi; the North American section of this study is being developed under the direction of the Central Department of Evangelism of the National Council of Churches.

Library of Congress Catalog Card Number: 64-23080

Printed in U.S.A.

75 cents per copy

Distributed by the Department of Publication Services
National Council of the Churches of Christ in the U. S. A.
475 Riverside Drive, New York, N. Y.   10027

CONTENTS

INTRODUCTION

INTRODUCTION

Already in the New Testament there are indications of acceptance of a continuing missionary calling in the secular world of 'principalities and powers.' Ephesians and Colossians point to this, as does the Epistle to the Hebrews, and the vision of the Christ saying to his people 'come,' not from the Holy Place in the Sanctuary, but from the agonies and abuse of the world 'outside the gate.'[1]

The response to the study on "The Missionary Structure of the Congregation," initiated by the World Council of Churches at its Third Assembly at New Delhi in 1961, has exceeded all expectations. *Where In The World?* (a study book by the present author, to introduce the subject to ministers' conferences and local congregations) was published in a first edition of 20,000—not without strong fears that the number was unrealistically optimistic—and sold out in four months. It continues to sell at a comparable rate, and the significant fact is that a good percentage of the number is for use in local congregations or in local ecumenical groups; and the express purpose of these groups is the reexamination of the missionary calling of the people of God. To take one example. A group of laymen in the United Church of Christ in Milford, Connecticut, undertook a study of the book, and at the end produced a Report calling for congregational action. One of the ministers wrote: "They stuck it

---

[1] "Structures For A Missionary Congregation," A Study Book for East Asian Churches, by John Fleming and Ken Wright, p. 49. (Unpublished draft: February 1964.)

out, although it was pretty tough going for most of them. I am sure that the Report as it stands does represent fairly closely the stage these laymen have reached at present. Almost every word, and certainly every idea in it, has been wrestled over these last few weeks, in true Faith and Order Commission style."

When it became clear to the group that "the nature of the community we have to serve will determine to a large extent the kind of mission that will be relevant," and that "in seeking new forms of mission, adapted to fit changing needs of our world, we can expect to look beyond our centralized, traditional congregational life," they also became aware of the extent to which they were "unready for such adventures."

> When we tried to pinpoint areas of worldly need in our community we discovered our ignorance and inexperience. It is easy to make a conventional list of problems drawing on newspaper editorials, and to talk about accepted ways of handling them. But it soon becomes evident that we talk in terms of social work and not at all of redeeming power. When we try to go further a deep silence falls.
>
> We confess with concern that we do not know where to start. In this, we believe, we are no different from most other suburban church members. The reason for our ignorance is that we have not taken either our mission or our world seriously for a long time.
>
> Before our mission in Milford can come alive we will need to recognize the areas of need. For that to happen we need a deeper knowledge of ourselves and our world in the light of the Gospel, than we once thought necessary.

They did not stop there. They went on to insist that their training for mission now required more than study. "To learn how to carry out the servant role we must engage in service." The group therefore spoke first for themselves.

> We intend immediately to set about developing appropriate forms of Lay Community, in accord with the findings expressed in the Report and the Appendix;[1]
>
> Also, in the belief that it is our calling to set up new "centres of dialogue" in Milford, we intend to observe, study and experiment in order to discover appropriate ways of doing this. We will do all we can to encourage our sister churches in Milford to help us in this attempt.

The Report also recommends small groups on the basis of occupation, common concern or location, pledged "to meet regularly for a common meal, common worship and study; to engage regularly in a secret discipline of personal devotion and contemplation; and to embark upon specific tasks of Christian service and witness chosen by the whole group."

They proposed to the Church Board:

> That we strengthen our mission within the congregation by the appointment of street or area reporters whose responsibility it would be to report emerging needs in their locality to the church. This would lead not only to a more effective pastoral relationship to all members, but also in time to development of new and appropriate forms of mission.

A proposal to the Deacons and Deaconesses points to the central question of how to help the membership to become aware of themselves as those who because they belong to Christ, belong with him in his missionary task in all the world.

---

[1] The Report has been mimeographed by the Central Department of Evangelism and a limited number of copies is available from Room 736, 475 Riverside Drive, New York, New York 10027.

We request the Board of Deacons and the Board of Deaconesses of our church to arrange to meet with the Senior and Junior Ministers and the Director of Christian Education, to discuss the whole matter of Membership Preparation, and the allied question of integration of new members into the life and mission of the church.

A NEW MOOD

This is an illustration from one local congregation of what can only be described as a new mood that seems to be dawning at many places and at many levels of the life of the church.

We see it in the host of new experiments emerging in the life of the churches across Asia, and reported in a study book prepared for the member churches and councils of the East Asia Christian Conference.[1] Common to all these experiments, the authors report, are the following common features:[2]

• They share the view that the Church and its congregations exist for God's mission in the world, and not for themselves; and *they see mission as a redemptive penetration and involvement in a society in which they believe Christ is at work.*

• They share a sensitivity that *looks for church groups becoming* more obviously and manifestly *the first fruits of God's new creation in Asian society,* as a sign of His purpose in Christ that can be seen by, and interpreted to, the 'outsider.'

---

[1] "Structures For A Missionary Congregation: The Shape of the Christian Community in Asia Today," by John Fleming and Ken Wright.

[2] Italics mine. Quotations from Fleming and Wright, op. cit., pp. 96-97.

• They take seriously the shape and structures of society, and the changes that are taking place in them, not to apply some pattern of rigid church forms to a new situation, but actually to *let the forms of society shape the new forms of church life.*

• They emphasize not only the role of the Christian individual, but the importance of *the Christian community or congregation,* not as a religious or communal group set apart from the world, but in some real sense *the beginnings of that new humanity which God is creating in Christ within the world.*

• They share the emphasis on the place of *the laity in the secular world, as a front line of the Church's ministry,* and consequently the idea that the whole Church is engaged in mission.

• They also share the conviction that . . . *the set-apart ministers . . .* must *have as their primary responsibility the preparation and equipment of the laity for this daily missionary involvement.*

• In many of these signs, there is a new understanding and appreciation of *worship, as the total response of Asian life to God in Christ*—both in the sanctuary and in the secular world. This response or *leitourgia* (liturgy and service) must take shape not only in forms of church worship, architecture, music and art, but also in a new style of Christian living in the midst of the world and its concerns.

We see the new mood in the statement of a Roman Catholic Bishop from Steubenville, Ohio,[1] insisting that the

---

[1] Reported in *The New York Times,* March 9, 1964. In "Ave Maria: National Catholic Weekly," March 7, 1964, Bishop Mussio's article appears in full. He suggests that in leaving its static parochial centres, the church again "would be somewhat like the Ark following the Chosen People in their trek to the Promised Land."

modern parish is "hopelessly outdated" and in dire need of "complete, radical" restructuring. He insists that because of the changes in the living habits of people brought about by modern social and economic change, the church must change its structures to match the structures of contemporary human need.

> To remedy the situation, Bishop Mussio suggests that large clergy centers be constructed to supplant the big central parish plants.
>
> The priests would "fan out" to provide "a concentrated spiritual service to their flocks" by establishing worship places and instruction centres, he continues.
>
> These could be the parlor in a Catholic home, the ballroom of a downtown hotel, or a suburban theater auditorium . . .
>
> According to the Bishop, working deacons and trained laymen would carry on the routine duties of the parish, such as bill paying and preparing of reports.
>
> Schools would cease to be parochial, but become regional, the Bishop notes, and the priest free to perform his main tasks of teaching, sanctifying and "bringing Christ to his people."

We see the new mood also in the steady emergence of lay training centres, industrial missions, groups seeking to bring the centres of decision-making in the public world into dialogue with the gospel, and the imaginative and moving ministries which reveal an increasing sensitivity to the structured forms of need as they are produced by the relentless pressures of our urbanized technological society—ministries to drug addicts, to excluded minority groups, to demon-tossed teenagers, to school drop-outs, to the dispossessed.

As one receives from across the world the evidence of a

mounting feeling that the church must now be released
from its self-concern and find its life by becoming the servant body of Christ in the world, there arises the feeling
that we are on the verge of the long awaited new Reformation. We have been in the midst of a renewal of Biblical
theology for some time; but the renewal of theology did not
lead (as many expected) to renewal of church life. But now
there seem to be increasing signs of a renewal of obedience
—of commitment—and a willingness to move out from the
security of past forms to the shapes of contemporary need.
The theological renewal which marked the movement back
to the rediscovery of the roots of our faith is now being
marked by the movement forward to the discovery of the
'signs of the times' from which Christ is calling us to present obedience in the world.

HESITATION

But this is only one side of the picture. The other side is
marked by the deep fears that the presentation of the study
has encountered.

1. The suggestion that the present congregational structure is inadequate to the contemporary task of mission has
often brought forth deep resentment—far more often from
the clergy than the laity. One reason for the initial resentment is undoubtedly misunderstanding—based upon a feeling that when those who are participating in the study speak
of the *inadequacy* of the residence congregation, they are
really suggesting that the residential congregation must
now be *abolished*. Since no documents or statements issu-
ing from the study have suggested this abolition of the residence congregation, we must ask why this fear has been
expressed so regularly. Does the very existence of this
study bring out a hidden fear in many now working in the
residence congregations that the study may discover that

their form of present commitment will have to be abandoned? Does the study stir up the frightening thought that the missionary calling today is leading us out with Abraham into the institutional unknown? There is sufficient open expression of this feeling amongst theological students —a considerable number of whom are declining to enter the parish ministry on the grounds that the residence congregation is alienated from the true centres of the world's life— and amongst a wide variety of laymen to make it imperative for us to ask such questions as: What is the place of the residence congregation in the contemporary mission of the church in the world?

The deep fears that are awakened when the adequacy of the residence congregation is questioned are not to be explained just by the fear of being separated from our familiar church ways. Behind it apparently is the deeply rooted anxiety that any alienation of the churches from the primary association with the residence community will remove the last bulwark against the imminent collapse of *the family* into final chaos. Time and again those who have expressed strong resistance to the study have given expression to the view that the primary relationship of the church must *always* be to the family. It is from the family, they have claimed, that the values that create society emerge, and it is through the church's relationship to the family that the way is found for the radiation of the gospel out into the many structures of society.

To this problem of the relation of the church to the family we will return in Chapter I. Let me add here, however, that though the family-centred congregation can no longer perform many of the functions it fulfilled in the past, this does not mean it will be unimportant in the future. And again, considerable attention is needed to the problem of how we can move out from the traditional congregational centre to missionary obedience in the new sociological

arenas. A common criticism of *Where In The World?* is that
it fails to give adequate attention to this problem of transition. More attention is given to it here; but it should be
said that answers will be discovered only as many more
congregations follow the example of the people in Milford,
Connecticut, in asking what they must do to fulfill their
missionary calling in their own situation.

THE SOCIAL GOSPEL AGAIN?

2. A second major fear is that the literature of this study,
when it speaks of penetrating the public worlds—industry,
commerce, leisure, politics—is forcing the gospel outside its
New Testament range of concern, and is in danger of re-
peating the old mistakes of the social gospel. It is admitted
that in the New Testament we are told of a new heaven
and a new earth in which all things will be renewed in
Christ. But it is suggested that it is not the task of the
church to carry out the direct translation of the final goal
of the Kingdom of God into the social structures of secular
life. That final translation is the work of Christ when he
returns. Our task as a church is more humble. We are to
witness to Christ as King and Saviour; we are to reveal the
redeemed life of the Kingdom in the quality of our community life as the 'called out' people of God and in personal relationships with others—in the family, in relationships of employers and employees, and in servant love to
those whose needs come before us. But the New Testament,
it is claimed, does not place the state or secular institutions
within the realm of redemption. They are within the realm
of providence and are under law, not grace. New Testament
ethical instruction for Christians is personal, and it teaches
us to wait until Christ returns before his Lordship over the
secular world will be manifest.

This crucial question will be considered again in Chapter

II; but we must not allow it to pass here. It is true that the New Testament gives major attention to personal ethics, and questions of political and social structures are dealt with not as abstract questions, but only in the way they impinge on the life of the Christian community. But this does not mean that we are advised to leave these areas of life, which we are told must also be redeemed by Christ, out of the area of Christian witness and obedience. On the contrary. The reason the New Testament concentrates attention on the personal to the apparent exclusion of the structures of social life, is that Christ's call for obedience comes to us at the points of our responsibility. In the time of the New Testament Church, the absolutist state set specific limits to the area of political responsibility open to members of the Christian community. So also they were excluded from decision making in relation to major social structures like slavery or the economy. But *within the full range of responsible decisions open to them they were expected to reveal in their life the first fruits of the new creation in Christ.* So, for example, this included the need to reveal in their fellowship the power of Christ to break down the barrier between Jew and Gentile, bond and free, male and female, barbarian and Scythian—and it is apparent that their use of the area of freedom given them enabled them to suggest in their life political and social consequences that caused deep fears to arise in the minds of emperors, politicians, and business leaders. As history has moved on, Christians have found that the areas of responsible decision open to them have varied greatly. So today we cannot expect the same forms of Christian life behind the Iron Curtain as in the U.S.A. But we can expect that in both cases, the church will be given the means for showing forth the signs of the New Humanity in Christ in such a way that the world may become aware of the judgment and mercy of Christ as he calls us out of the old communities of exclusion, hostility, pride and selfishness into the Kingdom in which all are one in Christ.

THE NEW RESPONSE

Today we are within a world of rapid social change in which there is an incredible diversification of the areas of responsible decision. The church as an institution, discovering that its inherited forms have left it outside these emerging centres of commitment, is finding it very difficult to free itself sufficiently to be present in these areas of decision in such a way as to disclose within the life of the fellowship the signs of the New Creation.

At this point, however, we must confess to overwhelming problems. It is all very well to speak of the church involving itself in these new areas of decision: but in what way? Many shudder at the thought of the church as an institution trying to regain control of the world; and insist that the church can only truly witness to the Lordship of the humble Christ when it respects the freedom of the secular world from this institutional control. For that reason we often speak today of the 'scattered church' and of Christian witness being given to the laity in dispersion in a way that fully respects the autonomy of these realms from the church whose institutional task is to train Christians for their life in dispersion.

That there is real truth here we can acknowledge; but in this way also lie grave dangers. One popular metaphor speaks of the laity being trained to light their candles from the central candle in the church so that they may then spread out into the secular realms taking with them the light of Jesus Christ. But what if our task is to be not so much the *source* of light for the world by bringing it *from* the church, but to be those who are to discern the light that is shining in the darkness of the world? Then our task as the church is to be out there learning what Christ is doing in the world, and seeking to be his interpreting presence—

shining as lights by reflecting the continuing deeds of the living Lord as he is working out his purpose in the events of history.

THE MARKS OF GOD'S PRESENCE IN THE WORLD?

Here we seem to be at the heart of the theological problem of the forms of the missionary presence of the church in the world. What are the marks of God's presence in the world? How can we read 'the signs of the times'? How can we undertake the perilous task of judging what God is doing in the events of our time? How can we determine the ways in which the church is called to be present with Christ in what he is doing in the critical events of the day? How can we be given sufficient freedom from the relativities of history to witness to Christ's purpose for history? In Chapters II and III an attempt is made to explore these questions; but it must be emphasized that we are only at the tentative beginnings of a crucial task, and that here are questions calling for the urgent attention of our churches.

ABOUT THIS BOOK

This book is a follow-up study to *Where In The World?*. It is just that—a study book, the purpose of which is to help church groups take a further step in their search for the way of missionary obedience. The first three chapters take up three of the major theological questions raised in *Where In The World?*—drawing on the thinking of the World Council of Churches Working Groups in various parts of the world. Chapter IV then seeks to provide examples of missionary response—not to be copied, but as stimuli to creative responses, 'each in his own place'.

The Working Groups in the study on "The Missionary Structure of the Congregation" have been encouraged greatly by the responses to the request for local groups to report the progress of their study and of their own experiments in obedience. It is clear that the study will only perform its task if this local response widens and deepens. We would be grateful, therefore, if groups would continue to send in reports to the Central Department of Evangelism of the NCCC, 475 Riverside Drive, New York, New York 10027, or to the Department on Studies in Evangelism, World Council of Churches, Geneva 20, Switzerland.

A personal word. The substance of the first three chapters was delivered as the 1964 Alden-Tuthill Lectures at the Chicago Theological Seminary. I wish to thank President Howard Schomer and Dr. Fred Hoskins for their personal kindness on that occasion and for their permission to use the material in this form.

WHAT
IN THE WORLD?

1

THE STRUGGLE FOR
A 'PUBLIC' MINISTRY

It is a widely expressed theme in the New Testament that the coming of Christ into the world has introduced a restless ferment of ceaseless change. A new age has been brought into the midst of the old one. "The old has passed away, the new has come." (II Cor. 5:17.) This new life "in Christ" is radically different from the ordinary life men lead. Natural human communities erect barriers of prestige, or class, or culture, or race, or language; but "in Christ there is no Greek or Jew, no bond or free, no male or female, no barbarian or Scythian." Natural human communities are dominated by self-interest; but "in Christ each esteems the other better than himself." As a result the presence of this life of the new age means the introduction of a ferment of constant change into the human communities of the world (Col. 3:1-15; I John 3:2) and even into our relationship to the world of nature (Rom. 8:19-25).

THE CHURCH AS THE SIGN OF THE NEW AGE

But what is the relationship of the church to this new fermenting presence? The answer of the New Testament is that the Christian community is made up of those who by baptism have been given a direct participation in this life of the new creation. The life of the church, therefore, is meant to be an 'earnest' or 'firstfruits' of the final transformation. The world should be able to see in the life of the church 'signs' of the Kingdom of God. Of course, the New Testament makes it clear that often the church does not live up to its calling; but it makes it clear also that, as the community of the baptized, Christians live under the constant demand to be worthy of this high calling; and under the constant warning that because of their high calling 'judgment must begin in the house of God.'

Because of this calling to be the sign or firstfruits of the coming Kingdom, the very nature of the Christian community is to be open to the future, for its life is an embodiment of its hope. Consequently the true place of the church is in the midst of the changes of life, joyfully witnessing to the Christ who makes all things new; witnessing to Christ who is the Lord of history and who opens the way to the future by overcoming the principalities and powers which enslave us to the old—to the past. The place of the community of Christ is at the perilous moving edges of change where Christ is offering to men a participation in the life of the New Humanity.[1]

---

[1]Hendrik Kraemer, writing in the W.C.C. Youth Department document, "Youth, Wine, Wine-Skins," No. 7, October 1963, has an article "Some Theses on Indigenisation." In it he writes: "The Christian Church, if true to its nature, is a body of *expectant people,* who are sustained in all which they do by this expectation of the Kingdom of God. In other words, the true Christian dimension is the future and not the past. By this expectation that transcends history, but nevertheless leavens existence in the present, he calls his believers to the never-ending task of making righteousness, truth and mercy powers of life in the present dispensation of travail in order that signs of the Kingdom may become visible and operative in it. In this context 'Mission' is to be kindled and borne by this expectation and it means extending an invitation to join in it. The kerygma is prophetic and apostolic (Eph. 2:20) and therefore dynamic. God, as he is presented in the biblical witness, is not a creator of religious virtuosi, but a sender of prophets, of apostles, of simple witnesses and servants to his purpose and concern. The Church is therefore God's co-worker, who in reverent amazement about the miracle of its calling and in loving and joyful obedience, fulfills the double 'diakonia' of witness and service to the world. To put

It should be no surprise, then, that in the course of the early centuries major changes occurred in the forms of congregational life.[1] But in the light of the New Testament view of the church's place in history; and in the light of the history of vast changes in forms of church life, the real surprise is the relative failure of the church since the Industrial Revolution to respond creatively to the vast changes in human society. There has been very little development of the new forms of congregational life that would enable the church to be the sign of the New Creation in the midst of the 'public worlds' of our time.

The congregational form with which we are familiar—the residential congregation—assumed its present importance in the middle ages. It was a creative response to the relatively static social life that resulted from the placement of people in their allotted positions in particular communities. The response of the church was to place a church building in the midst of each community, and from that centre to seek to bring each life and every facet of life under the Lordship of Christ. In this way the church accepted responsibility for Christianising the whole of life—education, health, economics, politics. And since the whole

---

it in other words, her distinctive nature and calling is to be, howsoever imperfectly, *ambassador* of Christ, who has brought not only redemption but also reconciliation. If the Church denies or ignores this distinctive nature and calling and chooses for anonymity, she is converted into a perhaps highly useful humanitarian agency."

[1] In *Where In The World?* a rough beginning was made in Chapter I in the task of tracing the outlines of that story. A number of recent studies help in filling in facets of remarkable changes that line the road of the church's history. The book edited by Stephen Neill and H. R. Weber, *The Layman in Christian History,* gives many fascinating glimpses of the variety of congregational responses to the missionary tasks of different periods. Fleming and Wright in "Structures For A Missionary Congregation" give a valuable summary of the long story, pp. 51-69. We now need studies which will undertake a direct analysis of these changing congregational forms of life through the centuries.

of life was centred on residence, the basic form of congregational life was the residence parish.[1]

But now, since the Industrial Revolution, vast changes have been occurring in social structures. By a powerful centrifugal force, huge sectors of life have been spun away from the residence community. Industry, commerce, higher education, health institutions, politics, mass communication, leisure, have separated off into "worlds" of their own. And, in fact, this separation has now gone so far that sociologists distinguish between the 'public' sphere and the 'private'. What is left in the residence community as such, is the 'private' world of the family, with local politics and early education; while the vast 'public' world of business, industry, politics, communications and the rest has now developed its massive institutional structures in separation from the life of the home. The church, having kept its primary congregational form in the community of residence, is discovering that it has isolated itself at the periphery of a large part of life by being separated from the vast 'public' segment of existence.

THE CONGREGATION AND THE HOME

Many clergy seek to defend the present tenacious maintenance of the primary form of congregational life in the community of residence, as we have seen, by claiming that the home is still the real centre of life. It is here, the claim goes, that the real standards and values are formed. Thus by influencing lives at this focal centre, creative Christian influences will then radiate out into the public arenas. What is involved here?

We must not forget the fact that children do still grow up in the matrix of the home, and that to fail to provide a structured form of Christian presence in the community of

---

[1] See *Where In The World?*, pp. 4-15.

the family would be to abandon a vital centre where lives are being fashioned, anxieties met and decisions made. For that reason we can agree that "there can be no question that local church units or centers, geographically defined and oriented to residence and family life, will always constitute one manifestation of the church in the world."[1]

To speak of the vital importance of the family, however, does not mean that it must remain as the determining focus of church structure. At this point we must raise a biblical question, an historical caveat and a sociological question.

1. Is it true, biblically, that the primary relationship of the church must always be to the family? Of course the family is God-given; and of course the Christian church must seek to make the family an expression in miniature of the fullness of life in the fellowship of Christ. But when Jesus called the Twelve he created a new society—free to move freely across the range of varying human associations. When it was suggested that discipleship had to be subject to family ties, Jesus insisted that obedience to him took priority over all human ties. "Whoever does the will of my heavenly Father is my brother, my sister, my mother" (Matt. 12:50; and in Matt. 10:34-39 the same truth is spoken in much harsher terms!). Life in the Kingdom of God transcends *all* human associations. In transcending them, it is true, it offers to them transformation. In dying with Christ to our old relationship to family, or master or servant, or to the state, we are raised with Christ to new life in all these old associations. But for Christians the primary

---

[1] From "Experimental Ministries in The Church," The Monthly Newsletter About Evangelism for February/March 1964, written "by Members of the Parishfield Community" in Michigan, and published by the W.C.C. The paper explores the necessity for and the limits of the residential congregation.

relationship is to the Kingdom of God. All human associations are equally secondary. So it is that today we need to be free to die to all our culturally-given relationships to family and the many other human communities, in order to be given by Christ new relationships within them that will be for our time more truly the signs of life in the Kingdom of God.

2. An historical caveat needs to be added. For the last 1,000 years or so, the primary relationship of the church in the West has been to the community of the family. That was because in feudalism the whole of life centred around it; and from that centre the church could relate to the whole of life. But now we have witnessed a remarkable change in social structure. The old family structure has disappeared. Industrialization and urbanization have not only torn asunder the old complex family of grandparents, aunts and uncles, children and parents, replacing it by the single-cell family of parents and children; they have also torn asunder the old unity of private and public life in which the family was the centre of work, play, worship, education. Thus if the gospel is to be brought to us now in all aspects of our life, the single approach of the residence congregation is no longer adequate.

This requires the highly difficult task of freeing us from the emotional attachment to the *primacy* of the family-centred congregational approach. But until that happens we will not be freed to discover the true role of the church —not even in the residence community. Because we so often try to do the whole work of the church from there, we are failing to do the essential task that must be performed in that realm—that of bringing Christ's word of healing to the new form of the family that is now struggling to be born.

3. The sociological question is this: To what extent is the family now the centre from which values and decisions flow? Or to what extent, for example, do influences flow in

the opposite direction—from the outside worlds into the home? It would seem that

a) in terms of the family centre being the source for the creation of values that determine life in the public worlds, the "long distance influence" has become progressively weaker the further the technological revolution has gone. The separation of the public worlds from the world of the family has continued to increase, and the result has been an increasing separation of these worlds from the influence of the church. In plain fact, therefore, we must confess that church influence radiating from the home centre has not effectively penetrated these public worlds. We have only to remember, for example, as Wickham demonstrated in his *Church and People in An Industrial City,* that by and large (particularly in Europe) industrial workers have never been in the church since the Industrial Revolution, and the truth begins to become clear that unless we seek to approach men in their public worlds, the witness of the church will continue to be absent from many vital areas of our modern existence.

b) if we are to minister properly to family life we must take account of the powerful pressures playing upon it from outside and bringing about major changes in its form. For example, industrialization has produced the new forms of residential association—high rise apartments as well as the modern suburbs; it has also produced the astounding mobility of modern families (about one-fifth moving every year; and more and more fathers [and mothers] being travellers); it is opening the way to the age of leisure; it has produced television and radio with their powerful outside influence on values, attitudes, desires. The family is in the midst of major restructuring and we do not yet see what the emerging form will be. But if the church believes it has an important witness to make at this point, it cannot make it from the centre of residence alone. It must seek direct presence in the midst of those powerful forces that come from the public worlds and help to mould the emerging shape of the family.

Sociologists will continue to argue about the extent to which the home can provide values reaching out to mould the public worlds, and the extent to which the home is at the mercy of the pressures reaching into the family from the public spheres of mass communications, politics, industry, science. We need not wait upon an outcome. Witness to the Lordship of Jesus Christ must now be carried on directly in both worlds, each with congregational forms appropriate to the witness that is needed. If it should avoid the task at either end, the church will condemn itself to irrelevance. At the moment our energies are concentrated almost exclusively at the residence end, but surely Gibson Winter is right when he says that "a ministry to individuals and families in the context of residential association is no longer a ministry to society; in mass society, individuals contribute to decisions for the good or ill of the society, but they make these contributions through the managerial hierarchies, labor unions, community organizations, political bodies, and bureaucratic units which organize their lives."[1] It follows then that that church must find ways of corporate presence within the communities of decision if it is to witness to the new creation that Christ brings to us in the midst of the old world.

THE DIALOGUE BETWEEN THEOLOGY AND SOCIOLOGY

As the question of the relation of the church to the new sociological structures is followed, the problem of the nature of the dialogue between theologians and sociologists becomes more urgent. The sociologists are clearly needed to

---

[1] *The Suburban Captivity of the Churches,* Doubleday & Company, Inc., New York, 1961, p. 136.

help us understand the sociological structures of our time; but in the discussion in this study, theologians (biblical and systematic) have several times expressed the fear that the dialogue is in danger of taking a dangerous turn. Sociologists can describe, they say; but they must not prescribe. That is a biblical and theological task; for it is from revelation that we must decide how the church must carry on its missionary task in relation to those structures. The dialogue then, is not a dialogue between two equal partners seeking truth together; but between those who can bring an accurate description of the patient's symptoms (sociologists) and those who have the prescription (theologians) which must now be applied.

On the other side there are those who insist that it is much more truly a dialogue than this. Biblical theologians (and historical) gives us descriptions of the once-for-all revelation of God's purpose for history and later applications of it. But since the God revealed is the Living God of history who becomes known to us now, not only through the record of his action in the past but also out of the midst of his present encounters with us, we must see theology as occurring *in* the dialogue. Undoubtedly the once-for-all revelation is used by God *in* the dialogue to make clear to us the word he wishes to speak to us now; but it must also be said that it is only *in* this dialogue that the meaning of the once-for-all revelation for us is made clear. Unless we are prepared to risk the treasures of the gospel in twentieth century trade with the scientific knowledge of our time, we will find that we have simply buried the talent committed to us in the soil of the past, and have consequently brought forth no missionary fruit in the secular market of our time.

RESISTANCE TO CHANGE

We should not be blind, however, to the powerful forces that are resisting the search for the new forms of congregational life needed. It is not just that we hate to leave the familiar; it is not just that our massive building investments in the residential world are sapping our readiness to admit the need to take on our pilgrim identity again, and go out with Christ into the far country of the public world. There is, in this land, a still greater block, the powerful myth of the 'private'—the feeling that our 'real' life is not in those public worlds, but in the private world of the home. This myth lies behind the powerful bourgeois attempts to maintain, in the outer suburbs, the disappearing forms of family and community life. The business and political life of the outer suburbanite is separated from the home; but in this disturbing world of rapid transition, he still wants the feeling that the old-time values of the home abide; and that this abiding 'private' world is the real world—the eternal world to which he can retreat from the exciting but frightening world of rapid social change. In this attempt, bourgeois man has found in the church his main ally. It has gone with him to his separate residence world. It has assured him that the home is what really matters. And so, ironically, it would appear that it is precisely *because* the local church is *separated* from business and politics and the pressing problems of society in transition, that bourgeois man has found himself 'at home' in it. We therefore have this ironic but tragic fact, that in many instances the residence parish congregation is popular precisely because it is irrelevant!

But, of course, this loved myth of the 'private' has no ultimate staying power. It is useful for the moment, because it protects the bourgeoisie against the emotional demands of a social transition which they find too rapid for immediate adjustment.[1] But soon the prop will be found unnecessary,

---

[1] We need to seek a better understanding of this phenomenon. Undoubtedly we have a more phrenetic form of the same dynamism in the radical right—a Canute-like attempt to hold back the waves of social change that are undermining the security of their past world. And the

and the present type of residence congregation will need to be re-formed to be what it is meant to be: the presence of Christ with men at the points where their real life is lived. Nor should we blind ourselves to the fact that this alliance of the church with the 'private' world has already resulted in the alienation of large groups of people who have emotionally already left the 'private' world of the past and desire to find their life's meaning in the public arenas.

THE ALIENATED

The most celebrated example of a group alienated from the church has been mentioned already—industrial workers as a class to a large degree have grown up outside the traditional church structure. Their lives have largely centred around the routine rhythm of work and leisure, with their energies and anxieties focussing upon the corporate battle for wage scales, working conditions, and the changing modes of production which constantly make their future a prey to obsolescence. For them the church with its middle-class family-centered focus has never taken the rhythm of their lives into the liturgy of its concern.

---

church must seek to understand how we can speak to the need of man for a basic security from within which he can be free for change. Here the 'once-for-all' character of the gospel is vital. We do witness to a Christ who is the same yesterday, today, and forever. But so also he is the Christ who is bringing about revolutionary change as he brings to us the offer of participation in his true future. This double characteristic of the gospel requires us to ponder deeply the question: how can the church provide the symbols of permanence—of abiding life in Christ—from within which we are free to be the presence of Christ within the changes of the world? We are not without light here. See, for example, the way the liturgy provides a symbolic expression of the creative tension between the permanent and the changing offered to us in Christ, in the East Harlem Protestant Parish. (See G. W. Webber: *God's Colony in Man's World.*) This question will need to be kept at the centre of our study and experiments on new missionary forms of congregational life.

Now a second major group seems in danger of alienation. The trend with the rise of the cities, has been for the middle-class white collar and executive groups to move out of the heart of the cities and into the suburbs, leaving the centre of the city to the low wage worker. The church has moved out with the middle-class, whose confessed aim has been to maintain the central importance of home and family, even at the cost of considerable separation from the place of work. The result has been that the home and work have been divorced—and even more, the home has been divorced also from the effective centres of politics, from vital community decisions such as urban renewal and city planning, and from the major cultural sources which still have their home in the city. The result has been two-fold:

1. an increasing sense of dissatisfaction for many suburbanites who desire greater unity between the two divorced sides of their existence and who sense the need for more responsible participation in the political, social and cultural affairs of the city;

2. an increasing difficulty on the part of many men to maintain meaningful membership in a church whose concerns are focussed on the suburb and which therefore reflects the divorce which he feels as his central problem.

This sense of relative unreality of life in suburbia—the theme of many a novel, film, article and sociologist's survey—seems to be increasing, as evidenced by a trend to middle and upper-class high-rise apartments in the city. There can be sought the lost unity; the reconciliation between public and private. But to a large extent the returnees sever their connection with the church; for it is felt as a symbol of their lost wholeness, not as the hope of the restored unity between the 'private' and 'public' part of their lives. The church finding itself locked out of the apartments, seeks imaginative ways for finding entrance; but the real entrance that is needed is for the church to accept the call to seek the restoration of the lost wholeness of life.

Another example of contemporary alienation comes from Latin America, where many of the younger generation are leaving the church. Abandoning the traditional resignation of their parents in the face of a life of squalor and cruel injustice, they are beginning to centre their existence on the hope for new participation in life made possible by technology and now available to them through firm political action. Consequently, as Richard Shaull reports from Brazil, the youth are finding that the residence congregation tends to pull them out of the human situation. "The end result has been expressed in a radical way by young people in Brazil who have said: 'The more we participate in the life of the congregation, the more alienated we become from the real world in which we are convinced God has called us to live and witness.' "[1]

THE CHURCH'S SPACE PROBLEM

These examples of alienation from the church in its residence congregational form, force upon us the question:

---

[1] W. Richard Schisler in an article "Christians in Both Church and World: A Latin American Point of View," in *Laity* No. 16, November 1963, pp. 42-44, makes a similar point. "Many young people are asking themselves today if there is any reason to spend energies in a church programme which, even when radically redirected, seems not much more than a paliative in a society in need of total social reconstruction." Schisler does indicate the struggle of the churches—both Protestant and Roman Catholic—to break out of their "ghetto" mentality. "Both Christian groups are struggling as never before to become relevant in the world, realizing the failure of the past both in dealing with the world absolutistically and separatistically. For the first time, the Church in Latin America is assuming its role as servant of the world, for the love of Christ who came to serve and not to be served." Similarly we can report examples of the church in Europe and the U.S.A. seeking to break out of the isolation of the ghetto of the private world, both in relation to industrial workers and high-rise dwellers. These are the signs of hope: signs, however, still waiting to be read by the church at large.

what forms of congregational life are needed to bring Christ's presence to modern men at those places where their decisions are made, and where the fabric of their existence is being woven? To put it pictorially: today the church faces again a real *space* problem. For centuries it took this for granted. Its place was assured: in the centre of the community. And so it gave all its attention to *time*: from baptism to last rites it concentrated on redeeming the time of man.[1] But now we are being forced to look at the space question again. Where shall the people of God gather? The problem is now one of the 'placement' of Christian community. The church, which has taken its space for granted, now must rediscover its place in the new worlds of modern human relationships in order to discover how to witness to the Lordship of Christ in the non-residential worlds in which he has yet found no room.

This suggestion of the need for the church to rediscover its true place in contemporary society—and therefore its need to take *space* as seriously as *time*—vaults us right into the midst of the contemporary theological re-examination of the relation between redemption and creation. If it is true that we have not been sufficiently conscious of the importance of man's spatial relations in the world, and have thought too abstractly of man's life in terms of time, and of the need for his time to be redeemed, this may well be because we have not taken seriously enough the inseparable

---

[1] It should be pointed out here that the *space-time* metaphor is being used here from a limited angle.

From another point of view, the church has been too little concerned with time, and too much with space. Too little with time in the sense that it was concerned with the time-span of the individual on his pilgrimage to eternity, but not adequately concerned about God's purpose for history itself. Too much with space, in the sense that it was concerned with mastery of locality while often forgetting the changing nature of life that time was effecting within that locality. When we combine both ways of looking at the problem, it emphasizes the need to take *space-time* seriously as an inseparable concept.

relation between redemption and creation.[1] In the creation story God's first commandment to man is: "Be fruitful and multiply, and fill the earth and subdue it; and have dominion over the fish of the sea and over the birds of the air and over every living thing that moves upon the earth." (Gen. 1:28).[2] Man is placed in inseparable relation to creation, so that God's purpose for him, which has to be unfolded in time, is necessarily related to the world of space. Man must work out the true relationship of man to man within the fecund possibilities given by the world of nature.

---

[1] C. A. Coulson, the British scientist, suggests also that our failure to take the world of things and of space as seriously as we ought, also has put us in trouble with the concept of time. He illustrates this by reference to the visit of a group of Marxist scientists from Russia, who were surprised when Coulson spoke on the influence of the churches on British life. "One of them—himself a scientist—got up and said, 'I have been very interested in what Professor Coulson has said, and his account of the belief in God that lies behind British culture. But surely this is not a sensible view to hold now, in view of our new knowledge about the age of the earth. You agree that this earth on which we live is about five thousand million years old, and that human life is only at *most* five million years—responsible human life less even than one-tenth of this. So if we call the life-time of the earth one day, man has existed for less than one minute. Is it not absurd to suppose that God should be primarily interested in these new creatures? What was he doing during all those other aeons of unrecorded time? Is God so inefficient as all that? In your insistence on his care and love for human beings, you make him appear an incompetent and slow workman.' I do not know what others would have said (writes Coulson); I felt, as never before, the utter need for a valid doctrine of creation—of the worthwhileness of things. For my Marxist friend was right: unless God enjoys his creation, then there is no meaning, no value in our material universe." And I would go on: unless we take seriously not only man's time, but his relation to space, his world setting makes no sense. Coulson's article is in *Laity* No. 16, pp. 31-37: "A Secular World? —God and 'Things.'"

[2] In the Covenant with Noah this commandment of man's creation is renewed (Gen. 9:1); but now, since it must be fulfilled within the context of the fallen world, its fulfillment is possible only as man participates in God's redemptive action. See the next Chapter for the crucial question of the relation of creation and redemption.

In medieval society, this question of man's relation to the world of nature receded into the background. Redemption tended to be thought of as applying to *man in isolation* from his world; time was too often separated from space. But now we have been driven back toward the Biblical view of redemption, because the vast release of man's creative capacities in relation to the world of nature has exposed the hollowness of the view that separates man from nature, and time from space. The public worlds have arisen precisely because of this increasing mastery of man over nature. The worlds of science, industry, commerce, mass communications and leisure, are the worlds which have been created precisely by this developing mastery over nature. And now the need for the church to find a place in these new worlds, is the need to find a way to witness to Christ as the Lord not just of time but of space also; the Lord who redeems mankind, not from the world of creation but in his relation to the world of creation, as he fulfills God's original commandment: "Be fruitful and multiply, and fill the earth and subdue it."

THE MARKS OF THE CHURCH

This way of putting the question of the places where the people must gather, raises again the urgent question as to what makes a Christian congregation—or, in traditional terms, what are the marks of the church?

a) The traditional marks, in the orthodox Protestant tradition, are *the Word and Sacrament,* with the addition in the 'Catholic' wing, of the ministry as guaranteeing the apostolic continuity of these. And certainly we cannot doubt that these marks will still have their relevance no matter what new forms the congregational life of the church may need to assume. For still it is the same Christ to whose Lordship we must witness, no matter how changed the circumstances; and still the travelling provisions needed on the way are those that Christ himself has given. It is not therefore the need for Word and Sacraments in the life of the church that is questionable in the orthodox Protestant view. What is now questionable is the static framework in which these appear in the classical confessional documents. Their statement was "The church is wherever the Word of God is truly preached and the Sacraments duly administered." The mental picture they give is static. The church had a given place, and so for them the question was simply —Is the Word being truly preached; are the Sacraments being duly administered? As we saw, they could take the *place* of the congregation for granted in the sixteenth century; but for us that is no longer true.

And so we turn to a second traditional emphasis on what makes the church the church.

b) In the Pietist tradition, word and sacraments were again assumed to be essential to a true congregation; but already in their time the question of the church's relation to space was beginning to re-appear. The opening of the new world called the church into geographical movement, and so the Pietists began to re-assert the primacy of *mission* as the mark of the true church. In the classical Reformers, place was so completely taken for granted, that it was assumed the command to "go" was limited to the time of the apostles. Subsequent congregations, it was said, had a fixed responsibility to their place of habitation. But the Pietists recaptured the significance of the call to mission. The true congregations are those who are gathered into the company of Jesus Christ, and therefore are available to him for his witness in all the world. The Word and Sacraments (and therefore the ministry) have their meaning in that they nurture the servants of Christ. It was because they saw mission as primary, that the Pietists saw questions of church order and even of doctrine, as relative.

We will have critical things to say of Pietism a little later.

But surely at this point their witness is of great importance. Their dynamic view of the church brought under question the limited perspective of the classical Protestant view of the church. They broke away from the static view which depended upon 'Christendom' for its power; and they began to free the church again for its mission in the mobile modern world. It was Pietism which first began to free the Protestant churches, so that they could move out across geographical frontiers. It freed the church for modern, overseas missions and gave the first impetus to the ecumenical movement, as the church was forced to face the need for unity if it were to witness to Christ's one purpose to gather all mankind into his one family. But it is now becoming apparent that the reformation in the view of the true nature of the witnessing congregation begun by the Pietists is still incomplete. They saw the need for the church to be in motion across *geographical frontiers,* in order to witness to all men that there is one Lord. But they did not question the adequacy of the residential congregation. They faced the new reality of the maritime age and the opening of the new geographical worlds; but they did not yet face the reality of the industrial age and the opening of the new sociological worlds. And so we are now facing the need to see that it is an essential mark of the church not only to witness to Christ as Lord of all nations; but that the calling to mission also requires us to cross the *sociological frontiers* to witness to Christ as the Lord of all life.[1]

The church must then, in its form of life, reflect its mis-

---

[1] This is the reason why the International Missionary Council on becoming the Division of World Mission and Evangelism of the World Council of Churches began to bring 'home missions' together with 'overseas missions,' and to emphasize the fact that crossing geographical and sociological frontiers are both necessary factors in the church's mission; and that the churches now need to learn to see the unity of the missionary task. See the four Section Reports from the Mexico City meeting of the DWME, December 1963.

sionary calling. The congregation is an event of 'the last days.' As the pilgrim people of God moving on toward the hope of their high calling in Christ, they are called to be the sign or the firstfruits of the New Humanity. They are called to reveal the power of Christ to manifest his new humanity by breaking through the human barriers of nation, of class, of culture, of race, and to bring forth a truly human existence in which together we grow up into a new mankind in him. It is necessarily the nature of the congregation to be with Christ in this restless movement toward the end. It is called to participate in his transforming work as he offers to men the life of the new creation that comes to them as they discover his Lordship in the midst of the struggles and temptations of their daily life. The Pietists rediscovered the need to see the congregation as participating in Christ's mission to all the world. They still, however, limited that mission too often to man as a private 'spiritual' being. It is now our task to discover those forms of congregation that enable us to participate in Christ's mission to all the world, including the social worlds that now dominate our technological age.

It may well be that we are given here an important clue in our current struggle with the doctrine of the church. So far in the Ecumenical Movement we have dealt with the problem *from the inside*—speaking of the marks of the church. But here now we seem to be driven to look at the question *from the outside*—speaking of the marks of God's presence in the world; and of the calling of the church to be the missionary presence of Christ in such a way as to reveal to the world God's redeeming presence. If this is so—and I believe it is—it would appear that these two discussions must now come into full relation to each other. To ask, for example, about true preaching, due administration of the sacraments, and valid ministry today, without asking *at the same time* about witnessing to God's presence in history now (on the basis of the Word given once-for-all); about Christ's purpose to unite us across all our divisions at his one table; and about our calling to be the ministering presence of Christ in the midst of the modern shapes of need—would be to fail to speak about the church of the Living Lord.

c) This need to discover those congregational forms that will enable us to fulfill the missionary task of witnessing to Christ's Lordship within the sociological worlds of public life, brings us to a question that has had a large place in ecumenical discussions of ecclesiology—the question of the *ministries of the laity*. The true significance of this question is that we are beginning to see that the ministry of the laity is not just to be clergy help in the private world of the church. To an extent never dreamed of previously, the incredible emergence of the "second nature" created by science and technology, in which men are succeeding at last in subduing the earth and establishing their dominion over it, is calling for the discovery of genuinely secular ministries within the creation commandment. The Pietists saw the need for all Christians to be ministers, but because they spiritualized the ministry and saw it as witnessing to Christ's Lordship over the inner life of man, they still kept the ministries within the life of the church as essentially separate from the world. Now what is needed is the discovery of ministries to Christ's Lordship within the secular worlds of public life so that the whole of man's creativity can be brought within the shape of the New Creation in Christ.

THE SECULAR MINISTRIES OF THE LAITY

We must be aware of the fact that emphasis upon the ministry of the laity does not necessarily result in the training for and the releasing of laymen into their secular ministries in the world. Mrs. Birgit Rodhe, in describing the situation in Sweden, characterizes a tendency which is in evidence in many parts of the church. She speaks of the tendency to think of the church as its own world.[1]

> Our churches cannot quite escape the stamp of isolationism. They tend to speak to me as a layman in a way that would mean that my first loyalty should always belong to the Church, that is, *the Church should be my real world...*
>
> To illustrate this trend, I would like to mention a recent book entitled: "Laymen Take Responsibility," which has been prepared by a group of theologians and laymen and issued by the study organization of the Church of Sweden. It is intended to stimulate and direct lay participation on every level of the work of the Church. Though it is an excellent book in many respects, it reflects the dangerous trend to overemphasize the role of the laity in the organized life of the Church, and to neglect the task of the laity as the Church in the world. Whereas nine chapters of the book are devoted to the life within the Church, just two chapters deal with life outside, namely in the family, and at work. There is an overstress on church attendance. The underlying assumption seems to be that if only people come to church, all will be well. Hardly any thought is given to a re-examination of the preaching, teaching and worship services, to relate to the concerns of laymen in everyday life.

It must be confessed then, that even when we speak of the ministries of the laity we have difficulty in moving outside the familiar structures of church life to discover the secular ministries of the laity in the new worlds of technological society. Those who are making the effort soon discover that to pioneer in this unfamiliar territory confronts us with great difficulties. If we are to be the presence of

---

[1] *Laity* No. 16, November 1963, pp. 45-50.

Christ in these places, we soon see that we cannot simply transplant the familiar forms of residence congregation into these new realms![1] The world of the home is set in a leisure context, and in that milieu likeminded believers are able to gather in a permissive setting to worship, study, plan and carry out a wide variety of activities. But the public worlds are not voluntaristic: they exist for particular purposes, and are by nature 'neutral' in that they bring people together across ideological differences in a common secular pursuit. There seems to be no room therefore—no space—for any satisfactory form of traditional congregational life.

For this reason, experimental approaches to discovering the right modes of presence in the public worlds centre on two methods:

a) drawing small groups together in their worldly context by using the areas of 'freedom' available.

b) gathering them together outside their public world,

---

[1] The need for discovering the way in which the church can be present in a secular world is causing a significant shift in Faith and Order discussions. "Order" until recently concentrated on the ordained ministry, the sacraments, and the internal structure of church life. Now such questions as the shapes of congregational life, the characteristics of Christian presence in the world, and the 'styles of life' appropriate to Christian witness in secular realms are coming into the discussion. These discussions find real rootage in the New Testament. It is significant, for example, that "in his appeal to 'order' in church life, Paul's word refers to the swift and efficient deployment of a troop of soldiers, as they get into battle formation. 'Order' does not refer to a static concept of the church, but to mobility and flexibility, and readiness for a battle." (Fleming and Wright, op. cit., p. 44.) But though "Order" discussions are in this sense returning to Biblical terms, it is true also that in another sense they are moving out into unexpected territory. The world of technological society is so much more complicated, and the freedom for Christian witness so much more extensive, that it is not surprising that even when we want to speak of these lay ministries and of the church ordered for its witness in the secular world, we do not know how.

but in such a way as to 'recreate' the context of that structure in order that their existence may be brought under the gospel.[1]

CHARACTERISTICS OF A
MISSIONARY COMMUNITY

At this point, the possibilities of inter-relationship with the congregation of the residence community are of great importance. It is, however, important to ask what are the needed characteristics of the gathered community—gathered either in the arenas of public life or in the private world of residence—if the laity are to understand and fulfill their ministry in the total mission of the church in the world. Fleming and Wright attempt a preliminary answer.[2]

> The basic demands appear to be three:
>
> (i) That the congregation is able to discern the different gifts of the Holy Spirit, *charismata,* given to its members. Keeping in mind the basic fact that the primary ministry in the Church is Christ's ministry, and that this is given to the whole body of Christians, congregations must act on the assumption that there are many gifts of the Spirit available in its fellowship, and that they are, in one way or another, for mission. There must, therefore, be some 'normal' patterns of the congregation's life that will function to 'discern the gifts of the Spirit.' In a rural community, this may mean discerning gifts of leadership or humble service in some aspect of rural life, or in the creation of community in a village, or the gift of wise counselling. In industry this might mean gifts that are able to reconcile

---

[1] The Evangelical Academies in Germany, the most sustained attempt on this level, are seeking to combine both approaches. In the Academy they 'recreate' the problems of public life, but in the field they also have teams working on the scene in industry and other areas of public life.

[2] Op. cit., pp. 124-125.

quarrels and misunderstandings, and create 'peace,' or it may mean gifts that help to clarify issues, to understand and express clearly the problems of both labour and management, or it may mean gifts that go far towards the solving of personal problems.

(ii) It follows from this that there must be structures in local congregations that function to train and develop these gifts, and in relation to the mission to be fulfilled by the whole Church in society. Many laymen are aware of their calling in this way. But they fail to find a Church structure to give them the help they need in relating the Gospel to the problems of trade unions, factory laws, labour and management, or the problems of industrial or rural communities in a fast changing society. The congregation must at this point create and offer structures of study, training, development of *charismata*, not in isolation from the world but in relation to its every-day life.

(iii) The congregation can then be a group that is deployed in the world in the various natural structures of society, with an understanding of the Christian message, an understanding of their society and its problems, and, in the case of different members, with a varied 'specialist' understanding of the particular problems of different sectors of society, and a Christian approach to them, though not with any ready made, cut and dried 'answer to problems.'

All this assumes, of course, a 'missionary congregation' aiming to work with God in His world, and seeing the world as its 'proper milieu,' and its gathering as a church in worship, in Word and Sacrament, as preparatory to, or better, complementary to, its scattering in the world in mission. This approach also assumes an understanding of the Church as the whole body of Christians, no longer relegated, as in the Middle Ages, to the role of passive spectators of the Mass, or as in the Reformation, to the role of passive audience of the sermon, but now primarily understanding themselves as called by God to share with Him in what He is doing in His world.

QUESTIONS

1. What is the nature of the new life "in Christ"? (See II Cor. 5:17-21; Col. 3:1-15; I John 3:1-3; Romans 8:19-25.)
2. If the church is to be the "sign" or "firstfruits" of the coming Kingdom, how can·its life embody its hope and be open to its real future?
3. How can the church minister to our private lives and also minister to our public worlds of business, industry, politics, etc.?
4. What church structures are called for by the needs of the residence community? What church structures are needed in the spheres of public life?
5. What groups of people are largely alienated from the church as it is presently constituted?
6. How should the laity be prepared for their ministries in the world?

2

THE UNRESOLVED DEBATE: WHAT IS GOD DOING IN THE WORLD?

At the Mexico City meeting of the Division of World Mission and Evangelism in December 1963, the work of Section III centred on "The Witness of the Congregation in Its Neighbourhood." There was no difficulty in reaching agreement on the need for a new definition of 'neighbourhood.' The final Report affirmed:

> 'Neighbourhood'—those near us, who therefore have a claim upon us—must be defined today not simply in terms of residence. In our mobile world lives impinge upon each other in an increasing variety of "worlds." Thus, for example, in modern cities and suburbs our lives often are intertwined less with those who reside near us than with those who are "given" to us in other communities such as work, or recreation, or politics.
>
> The variety and mobility of these increasingly important non-residential neighbourhoods, gives new dimensions to the task of Christian witness. It suggests the need for new forms of congregation. It underlines the need to discover the essential unity of the mission of the church in relation to the mobile variety of modern

29

communities. It daily makes more absurd our denominational divisions which cut across the unity men are given in these natural communities.

When an attempt was made, however, to explore the nature of the Christian witness that is required in these non-residential neighbourhoods of public life, a deep difference soon appeared. The majority felt obliged to affirm that the witnessing task of the church requires it "to watch for the signs of Christ's presence in the communities of the world," and to be ready to join with Christ as he carries on his redeeming work within the events of contemporary history. "The church should seek for the gift to interpret what is happening now in the events of world history on the basis of God's particular work in the history of the events recorded in the Bible." The appropriate forms of witnessing life for today will appear, the majority concluded, when Christians "take the incarnation seriously," "by serving and suffering—through involvement in the arenas of the world's struggles not only as individuals, but as old and new forms of congregation." Christians are those who, believing in Christ's Lordship over the world, watch for the signs of his redeeming work wherever they appear, and stand ready to join him where he is at work bringing forth the signs of the New Humanity. "Thus," the Report affirmed, "we see the significance of Christians from a city church in Taiwan going out into the police stations, trade unions, government offices, and finding that 'in these encounters they find a shape of Christian obedience being written for them by what God is actively doing in the structures of the city's life outside the church.'"

THE 'EXTROVERT' CHURCH

The Report then pointed to the need for the church to abandon its present separated existence, and affirmed that

perhaps the big breakthrough on the road to unity will
come only as our divided congregations together turn
from their introverted life and seek to find unity of
witness within the secular communities of the world.
. . . The New Delhi Assembly spoke of the need of the
churches to take "responsible risk" and to be ready to
face the possible dissolution of past forms as we reach
out to the true unity that is Christ's will for us. We
would affirm the need for "responsible risk" in reaching out to the congregational forms needed if we are
to be true witnesses to Christ in the contemporary
world.

With much of this, the minority agreed. That God is at
work in the world they agreed. That the church is called
to cooperate with God in that work they also agreed. But
what is the nature of God's work in the world, and what
therefore is the nature of our ecclesiastical response? The
majority affirmed that Christ is at work in the world carry-
ing out his reconciling work. In the 'secular conversion' in
Latin America, where the masses are at last awakening and
turning from despair to hope and from resignation under
injustice to a determination to build a society where all
men will have a new dignity and a freer participation in a
more truly human community, the majority saw the signs
of Christ's redeeming work.[1] Therefore they affirmed the
need for Christians to be in that struggle, interpreting
Christ's redeeming purpose to their neighbour by word and
deed, and forming congregations at the points of struggle

---

[1] A remarkable address was given at the Mexico City meeting by
Gonzalo Castillo-Cárdenas, which graphically describes the way the
church in Latin America is being called to undergo a radical change in
response to what God is doing in the secular events of their contemporary life. Here are some of his key statements: He spoke of the
"infancy and childhood of the Protestant movement" in describing the
expansion that has occurred in the evangelical churches in Latin America over the last century. It was characterized by a strong sense of sep-

so that as they work in this secular setting, they may live within the interpreting Word and the sustaining Sacraments at the place where decisions must be made and obedience must be sustained.

PROVIDENCE AND REDEMPTION

To this the minority objected. They believed that we must see this work of God in the world as God's *providential* work, not Christ's *redeeming* work. Christians should be there in those struggles, but as individual citizens fulfilling their secular obedience, not as Christian congregations wit-

---

aration from the world and a "neglect of the political and social aspects of the evangelistic mission."

Now, however, the events of the world are bringing about a crisis in the church.

"The Latin American people are biting into a task of demolition of an evil social and political order whose beneficiaries are trying to protect it at all costs. . . This very belief actually constitutes a marvellous conversion from fatalism to hope, from indolence to revolutionary action, and from resignation to rebellion.

"In the middle of this revolution-in-process the Christian suffers as he is besieged by agonizing decisions. Should he isolate himself, take refuge in personal piety, flee contamination in search of his own salvation? Or ought he better intervene in the situation in order to help avoid an abrupt change, seeking to preserve the established order with the hope of being able—gradually—to purify, improve, and humanize it? Or should he perhaps give himself over heart and soul to a revolutionary program proving his loyalty to the gospel by his identification with this program or party?

"These questionings are inextricably bound up with the church's work of evangelization, with its Christian service, with its corporate life, that is, with its total mission. But the churches find themselves desperately short of the theological and Biblical reflection, the social ethics, with which to respond coherently to the agonizing questions of their members, especially their youth, when Marxism seems to offer answers and specific remedies to the burning problems of the moment. In every corner of the church there is perplexity, confusion, disorientation. Many Christians, whose consciences have been sensitized by the preaching of the gospel—many of them seminary students—have chosen to abandon the church and become communist leaders. Others find that their loyalty to the Word of God requires them to participate *as Christians*, both in the demolition and in the construction, running all nessing to God's redeeming work. The minority expressed the belief that to see God's work in the world as Christ's redeeming work calling the church into existence at those points, would result in the dissolution of the necessary distinctions between the church and the world, between church and state, between grace and nature. And so the report drew attention to this vital conflict in these words:

> The discussion raised a theological issue which remained unresolved. Debate returned again and again to the relationship between God's action in and through

---

the risks and living with all the ambiguities of the revolution. In doing this they have suffered rejection by their elders and frequently by the hierarchy of their churches. The Protestant Christian in Latin America now lives with this agony. It is the price of living 'in the midst of the times,' where the voice of the Lord is heard: 'See, I have set you . . . to pluck up and to break down . . . to build and to plant . . . for I am with you, says the Lord, (Jer. 1:10, 19). But, how shall we obey the Lord concretely in these days?"

A similar interpretation of the situation of the church in Latin America is given by Richard Schisler (in *Laity* No. 16). Speaking of the rapid growth of Protestantism in the nineteenth and early twentieth centuries, he writes: "Conversion to Protestantism meant a break with established mores and the necessary choice of a new community—the local church—around which to build relationship. Out of this grew a 'ghetto' mentality which, at the same time, was a bane and a boon. A boon for it strengthened the sense of community of the faithful and made it bolder in proclaiming the faith; a bane, for this mentality meant a clear break with the world."

Might it not be that here we see the "moments" of God's dealing with his people—that in this period of secular despair, he was building up the separate community with a new sense of dignity, of belonging, and of the life of the Spirit; and that now he has moved in the world of secular events to bring forth a new hope, and is calling for a new movement of his church from their 'separate' existence to join him as his witnesses in the world of revolution. The big question now is: is the church ready to move out into the world with him? And that question is appropriate not only to Latin America! Schisler believes that there are strong signs in Latin America that this movement of obedience is beginning to occur. "For the first time, the Church in Latin America is assuming its role as servant of the world, for the love of Christ who came to serve and not to be served."

the church and everything God is doing in the world apparently independently of the Christian community. Can a distinction be drawn between God's providential action and God's redeeming action? If the restoration and reconciliation of human life is being achieved by the action of God through secular agencies, what is the place and significance of faith? If the church is to be wholly involved in the world, and its history, what is the true nature of its separateness? We were able to state thesis and antithesis in this debate, but we could not see our way through to the truth we feel lies beyond this dialectic. Yet we believe that all attempts to adapt the structures of the thinking of the church to match the great changes that are taking place in the world will be doomed to paralysis until we can find the way through to a truer understanding of the relation between the world and the church in the purpose of God.

If this statement of the issue is correct, and I believe it is, then the question of the congregational forms appropriate to our contemporary witness depends upon a solution to this question of the relation between God's work in the church and his work in the world. Is it proper to distinguish these as his redeeming and his providential works? This connects immediately, of course, to the question of the relation between creation and redemption, and the relation between Christ's Lordship over the world and his Lordship over the church. Can we break this deadlock?

THE BREAKTHROUGH?

I believe that the break is already occurring, and that we are beginning to see the issues involved here:

1. There is *the historical question of confessional formulation*—a factor that is still considerable in the European

established churches. In the period of Christendom and the State church, a working relationship had to be established between the church as an institution, and the state as a fellow-institution. Hence the doctrine of the two arms —Church and State; with their two realms—grace and nature; and their two weapons—Word and sword. Both, however, were seen as being directly and consciously responsible to God. The Christian church and the Christian state cooperated in the work of God, within the tension established by the definition of their distinguishable but interrelated spheres. It was then, in this setting, that the confessional statements of the Reformation were made.

Now, however, that setting is increasingly disappearing. Less and less does the state see itself as directly and consciously responsible to God, and as a partner of the church; and as this dissolution goes on we are beginning to see that this distinction of the two spheres was dependent upon the Christendom situation. In the New Testament, the church is not a separate sphere or place. Instead the church is the gathering of those in the world who have been given a different apprehension. They gather wherever the world brings people together, to witness to their fellow human beings of God's purpose for his creation and the Lordship of Christ over the world. The church is, therefore, wherever there is this awareness of Christ's Lordship and wherever there is a readiness to be the servants of the Lord.

With the dissolution of 'Christendom' and the rise of our modern industrial society, life again has become so mobile that the medieval concept of the state once more is dissolving and the visual image of church and state as two partners standing side by side in related but contrasted realms of conscious responsibility no longer reflects our real situation. Now there is the whole network of institutions caring for the secular life of man (of which the state is one), and if the church is to train her members to be the servant presence of Christ within this varied world of public life, it must be admitted that they can no longer be reached by a church that accepts a definition of its place as being in a separate sphere. In Christendom all areas of public life could be reached from the separate church sphere. All persons belonged by law to the church; the church had direct connections with all aspects of public life; and life itself was relatively unified in the world of residence with the church at the centre. Because all of these conditions have now gone, the church must give up its assumption of its separate sphere and free itself for access to all areas of the life of our mobile world.[1]

2. There is *the theological question of the relation between creation and redemption.* The working distinction between the providential and reconciling works of God that was accepted in classical Protestant thought (and particularly in Lutheran theology) made sense in a situation where the state was given responsibility for part of God's

---

[1] We have referred already to the struggle in Latin America for the church to break out of its 'ghetto' and to take up its servant work in the world. That problem, however, is not just a Latin American one. It is true in Europe, and in the U.S.A., largely because of the historical factors mentioned here, and it is documented in *Where In the World?*. An indication of the world-wide character of this problem, and of the growing awareness of it is the following statement from Fleming and Wright, p. 68-69.

". . . generally speaking, the congregation in Asia today is in both sociological and religious captivity.

"It is in *sociological* captivity, because it has inherited from the missionary movement patterns of life which grew up in a different society and culture (and which even in that society are no longer relevant), yet these patterns are accepted unquestioningly as a necessary and fundamental part of the Church's life, which must be reproduced wherever the Church is planted, and the congregation gathered. The structures of the Church are unrelated to history, and to the particular society or community structure in which the congregation now lives.

"It is in *religious* captivity, because the essential task is thought of as either the gathering of individuals into a religious community unrelated to the natural communities of life, or as the provision of remission (providence), and the church for the other side of it (redemption). But as we have seen, this working arrangement is now breaking down. The breakdown has forced us again to look at Biblical teaching at this point, as we are discovering that a much more dynamic relationship between these two aspects is there assumed. Barth's double dictum that "creation is the external basis of the Covenant," and "the Covenant is the internal basis of creation," is an apt summary of the Biblical position. Old Testament scholars have made it clear, for example, that it was through God's *redeeming* work that Israel came to their understanding of God's *creative* work. Undoubtedly there are distinctions between's God's providential and redemptive works, and between Church and State. But Church and State do not have different spheres—with providence serving the material and redemption the spiritual. Providence and redemption are equally related to creation, and the secular institutions such as the state and the church both serve God's redemptive purpose for creation, in distinguishable, but complementary ways.

---

ligious ordinances for those who feel the need of them, and come to church to get them. Structures of the congregation are directed to these ends, and the relation of the congregation to the ordinary life of society is seen only in terms of individual goodness and piety, and not as something which must be expressed in the style of Christian living and in new forms of the Church's life.

"The paradoxical result of this dual captivity of the Church is that while the impact of the Gospel has been a major factor, both directly and indirectly, in the Asian social revolution, yet the churches as institutions find themselves on the fringes of that revolution, and seldom in the mainstream of the development of the new national communities of Asia. The structures and assumptions of the churches seem to hinder them from becoming involved in the social changes, for which their Gospel is in many respects largely responsible.

"There can, therefore, be no more urgent task than this: that in Asia, where the new social structures of an emerging society are in the process of formation, the Church should now find those structures for her own life, which will enable her to be seen as the first fruits of God's reign within that society."

We have seen how, in the creation story, God commands man to subdue the earth and bring forth its full creative capacities. In the fall story that follows not only is man's relation to himself and to his human partner distorted, so also is his relation to nature. But God's promise of redemption includes the full restoration of man to himself and to his neighbour within the restored relationship to nature. And so when Jesus comes announcing the Kingdom and when by his miracles he outlines the shape of the Kingdom, it includes the restoration of man's relationship to nature. Jesus walks on the water as the sign of his Lordship and in breaking bread in the miracle of the feeding of the 5,000 brings forth the full expanding fecundity of nature in the service of man (John 6). And so in Colossians (particularly 1:15-20), in Ephesians (particularly 1:9-10), in John's Gospel (particularly the prologue), and in Romans 8, Christ's redeeming work is set forth in the full framework of man-in-relation-to-nature.

THE CHURCH IN TENSION WITH THE WORLD

What then is the role of the church? Does it have a separate role from other human institutions? The church is seen in Paul and in James as the 'sign' or 'firstfruits' of Christ's purpose for all creation. The church is the community of those who have become aware of Christ's redeeming work, who confess his Lordship, and seek the way of direct obedience. They do have a separate life. But that is because the way of the world is normally one of disobedience to Christ; and therefore when as Christians they gather to acknowledge Christ's Lordship over his creation and to witness to him, they find that they are in tension with the way of the world. But this does not mean that the church has a separate sphere: a separate segment of life from the segments for which the other institutions of the world have responsibility. The separate life of the church is in the world and for the world; and the life of the church is meant to be seen by men as the sign of Christ's purpose for all life: as the 'firstfruits' of Christ's redeeming purpose for his whole creation.

The tension between these two aspects of the life of the church—its life as a separation from the way of life in our ordinary human communities; and its life as the sign and foretaste of God's ultimate purpose for human communities—is reflected in the images of the church in the New Testament. On the one hand, the church is described as a community of aliens and exiles whose citizenship is in heaven; but on the other hand, it is spoken of as the light of the world, a letter for men to read, the servant people, the salt of the earth. The nature of this tension is important, however. These are not balancing truths. The ultimate meaning lies in the second series. The 'separation' is a preparation for the 'engagement'; the separate life is the basis for the servant life.[1] In other words, the church exists for the world.

For this reason, in John's vision of the final existence there is no temple. In the new heaven and the new earth, the separate life of the church will have dissolved, for Christ will be all in all. Similarly, the Christian faith witnesses to the withering away of the distinction between the sacred and the secular. Finally there will be no need for separate prayers; we will be immediately conscious of God's presence and will pray without ceasing. In the meantime, however, the church is needed as the disciplined and nurtured body of separate witnesses to God's redeem-

---

[1] Sometimes these two aspects may be separated in time, as in Latin America where the time of 'separation' is now giving way to the time of 'engagement.' Today it would seem that they must be held in conscious inter-relation, with a conscious concentration on the need for the laos to be trained for engagement.

ing purpose for all creation.[2] At the same time it must constantly be fighting against the tendency for the tension between the church and the world and the sacred and the secular to fall into separate spheres. The separate is meant to be the sign of God's purpose for the whole. The church like the Incarnation is meant to be the truly 'secular' event. In it the world is meant to see its true future. In it the overcoming of the separations, divisions and hostilities that are the sign of our fallen life are to be shown forth. And if the church is to fulfill that missionary task today, how else can she do it than by her presence at the points of separation, division, and hostility, at the places where the reconciling power of Christ is most needed? When we see this need for the church to be the 'sign' of Christ's Lordship in all creation; being available to Christ as his witnesses by deed and word, wherever he is bringing forth the life of the

------

[2] In commenting on Bishop J. A. T. Robinson's 'secular Christianity,' Father Herbert McCabe comments: "His goal is the entirely acceptable one of Christianity without religion, but he differs radically from traditional Christian thought in supposing that this aim is to be achieved by human reorganization rather than by the second coming of Christ. Religion, he quite rightly observes, depends upon a distinction of sacred and secular. Certain things, places, actions or people are 'sacred,' set apart from the common life; this is the necessary condition for cult and religion. Undoubtedly the consequence of the incarnation is the abolition of a real distinction between sacred and secular, the religion which was central to the Old Law was fulfilled and transcended in Christ, but the absolute identification of the common world with the sacred must await the consummation of the kingdom to which we still look forward. The withering away of the Church which we await so impatiently is a feature of the *parousia,* where there will be no temple in the city 'for the Lord God Almighty and the Lamb are its temple.' For traditional thought we are in an intermediate era in which, while the new world is founded in Christ's risen body, we are not yet visibly and gloriously members of that world. The last things are not wholly to come as they were in the Old Testament, nor yet wholly realized as at the last day; hope is still an essential aspect of our divine life. Now it does not seem that the Bishop maintains this difficult tension between realization and hope." *The Honest To God Debate,* The Westminster Press, 1963, pp. 176-177. Quoted by permission.

new creation; we must be aware, however, of two major dangers.

1. There is the danger that as we see the signs of Christ's redeeming presence in the world outside the church, we will obliterate the line between the church and the world, and define the church simply as wherever God's redeeming work is being done. But this will not do. There is the need always to call those who are working within Christ's plans to a conscious awareness of their Lord, and to a direct obedience to him in word and deed. The church is wherever men are being gathered into his name.

But further, the Cross stands as a constant reminder that the witnessing relationship of the church to the world always includes the element of 'scandal,' the likelihood of "offense"; and therefore a fundamental tension in which the church has to struggle against the temptation to compromise her gospel in order to remove the scandal and find a false basis of harmony—peace, peace where there is no peace. Bishop Ignatius Hazim of Lebanon has drawn attention to the danger that in the search for relevance and participation in the life of the world we may forget that the focal source of mission is that of Christian genuineness—refusal to conform or compromise, and recognition that we must, as the Lord did, sanctify ourselves for others. In this period before the consummation, that tension between the church and the world will never be done away. "Christ was the problem two thousand years ago, and he remains the problem today; the Cross is still the eternal challenge which does not allow for compromise."

2. There is also the terrible danger of failing to see the equivocal character of the signs of Christ's presence in the world. Yes, Christ is there—in the revolution of our time—offering new life, new hope, new humanity. But Christ is present, as he always is, offering in that situation the op-

portunity for true life and he offers it as the gracious one: "Come unto Me." And that means that there is also the terrible possibility of misusing this gracious gift, by grasping the freedom he is offering and turning the opportunity into demonic directions, thus coming under the sway of principalities and powers. For this reason there is the urgent need for direct Christian witness, and the pressing task of gathering of Christians around the Word and Sacraments at the places where the important decisions of life are being made.

THE CHURCH FOR THE WORLD

Here we see the importance of the discussion of the relationship of God to the church and to the world. George Casalis has stressed the need for us to reverse our normal assumption about the order of these words.[1] We normally think in the order—God-church-world; as though God is primarily related to the church and through it to the world; and also as though God relates himself to the world through the church in order to gather everyone possible from the world into the church. We must learn to reverse the order, says Casalis, to God-world-church. God's primary relationship is to the world, and the church exists for the world. The church is the fellowship of those who can speak to the world of God's purpose for it and presence in it; because they know Christ as Lord of the world.[2] The church is the fellowship of those who are ready to serve the world by

---

[1] See *Where In The World?*, pp. 76-80.

[2] At this point the church is not as well trained as it ought to be. As the Japanese theologian Masao Takenaka puts it: "Theology in the last few centuries . . . has been primarily the domain of theologians who contemplated the meaning of the activities which take place within the church building. We must enlarge the scope of theology in order to discern the redemptive and transforming work of God in the whole cosmos through the study of our concrete involvement as the people of God in the world." (*Laity* No. 16, p. 19.)

being the obedient presence of Christ at the points of the world's true need. For this reason, then, the church sees itself not as a separate sphere, but as the people of God in the world taking their form around the changing shapes of the world's needs. Casalis would not suggest that the church does not need its 'separate' existence.[1] It does need to gather around the Word and Sacraments. But these too exist for the world. Thus the Word is not truly preached unless it is in dialogue with the world's needs; nor are the Sacraments duly administered unless they take on their true character as living signs of God's gracious salvation

---

[1] It would seem wise here to distinguish between different meanings of the word 'separate' in this connection. Its meaning in this sentence is the simple one of temporary separation from the daily world, for worship and study and training, for return to the world as witnesses and servants. In this sense 'separation' and 'engagement' belong to each other and are as inseparable as breathing in and breathing out. It must be confessed that too often there is a failure of engagement—because the church works harder at its 'come' structures than at its 'go' structures. In the New Testament "Come" is there all right; but it is not "Come to church"; it is "Come to *him*—to that living stone." It is "Come unto Me." And those who come to Christ are then yoked to him so that they must "Go" with him into all the world. So the church's 'separation' is preparatory to its 'sending.'

There is however a second meaning of 'separate'; in the stronger sense of the development of a community which is in marked tension and conflict with the world, so that its separation is more than a gathering in preparation for sending; it is a permanent sign of "offense." The 'sect' groups put their emphasis on this second meaning of 'separation' and believe that in this age, the necessary conflict between the community of Christ and the communities of this world is such that always the church must stand over against the Kingdoms of this world calling for the radical separation of believers by the straight gate of repentance that leads from the broad roads of the worldly communities on to the narrow road that leads to life eternal.

Who can say when the church is required to give greater emphasis to this second relation to the world? The 'sects' stand as a constant reminder of the danger of compromise; but they stand also as a constant temptation to avoid engagement. In each situation the church is required to judge its friendship with the world to see whether it is compromise; but it is also required to judge its separation from the world to see whether it is a failure to be with Christ in his work in the world.

coming into being in his world. Thus to quote again from the Mexico City document on "The Witness of the Congregation in Its Neighbourhood":

> In all ages the church is called to be the sign of God's purpose for His whole creation. This unchanging calling in the changing world is expressed in the eucharist in which the redemption of the whole world given in Jesus Christ is offered continually for and to the world. Thus if the eucharist is the sign of God's redeeming work, its redeeming reality needs to be manifested within the broken world of the contemporary neighbourhood. Thus, when Negro, Puerto Rican, Anglo-Saxon share the eucharist together in a storefront church in East Harlem, the true secular significance of the event becomes clear. It is a sign of the power of Christ to make "one new man" from the broken humanity of our world.

TWO-WAY TRAFFIC

It is here that we see the main weakness of the Pietist position. They recaptured the understanding of the church as constantly involved in mission to the world. But always they saw God as moving through the church to the world. They insisted that first Christ speaks to the individual in the church, and then change moves from converted individuals out into society. The great Pietist Jakob Spener distinguished three areas of human life, the *clerical* (heirarchicus), the *private* (oeconomicus) and the *public* (politicus). God works from the church through Word and Sacraments (clerical) and moves through regenerating individuals by the Holy Spirit (private) into the world (public). It was the firm belief of Spener that if only enough individuals were converted all the problems of public life would be solved.

Two major fallacies underlie this widespread assumption:

1. It fails to take adequate account of the reality of continuing sin in believers. This naive assumption that converted people automatically become good citizens has been responsible for a major failure in the responsibility of the church to train members for their secular ministries in the world. It is, for example, unfortunately true that there has been an unending stream of conversions in states like Mississippi and Alabama for many years, but it can hardly be said that this stream has been unusually successful in solving the major problems of the public life of the area.

2. The Pietist assumption misinterprets the Biblical account of the way God works in the world. Their assumption is that God always initiates change from inside out—from inside the church and out into the world, and from the inside of the believer out into life. Neither of these assumptions is Biblical. God spoke to Israel through his action in outside events—so through the actions of a Cyrus and in the events of an exile, he called them to obedience. Christ called upon his followers to learn to read the signs of the times; and warned them that not only must they be ready to hear his call from the needs of the world—from the sick, the imprisoned, the hungry, the naked—but also they must confess that often 'outsiders' respond to his call before believers (Matt. 25:31-46). Often then, it is through the painful pressure of outside events that God calls us to face the need for a change in internal attitudes. A stark case of this at present is the race revolution. Here the church, far from being the source of the stream of creative change, now finds itself forced to face the need for painful changes inside the church and inside the believers, by the pressure of the changes God is bringing about in the outside world.

What does this mean for us? It means that we must throw off these false Pietist assumptions. We must learn again that God speaks to us from the events of the world, and calls *to* the church from the world. It means that we must learn to turn the life of our church inside out, so that we are ready to respond to the call of Christ from the world, learning to take our shape around his servant presence in the world.

GOD'S CALL FROM THE WORLD

Surely here the race crisis must be seen as the work of Christ in which the church is being called to undergo radical change. In this crisis we have seen the vast upsurge of oppressed peoples seeking dignity, justice and freedom. In this we can see the work of Christ offering to us the possibility of a society that is more open—one in which the dividing walls of hostility are broken through to an extent not previously realized. So also we can see the signs of Christ's redemptive presence in the struggle of Negro leaders to keep the revolution within the creative paths of love, with the recognition that the Negro by forgiving his white brother can offer him freedom from the strong chain of his guilt. And if it is true that the church is called to be the 'sign' and 'foretaste' of God's redeeming purpose for all the world, then surely there is here a clear demand for the church to answer this call of Christ from the midst of his work in the world. Here we hear his summons to new forms of church life—showing to the world our readiness to leave the segregated patterns of residence communities in which we have allowed ourselves to be imprisoned, and showing to the world our readiness to identify ourselves with Christ's work for a New Humanity by joining with him in the struggle against oppression and injustice, prejudice and hatred. By moving out to these new forms of congregational life in the midst of this struggle, we will tell the world that we know it to be the calling of the church to let the world see that community life in which Christ is breaking through the hostilities, prejudices, fears, and hatreds which mark the life of human communities. In this way the life of the church will then become a sign through which the world will know Christ's purpose for all mankind. If we argue that we are unable to do this; that it would split the church or cause strife; we show immediately that we do not believe that the church exists for the world. We show that we assume that the church exists for itself; and by this assumption the church continues to die of the sickness of self-concern, failing to heed the words of its Lord: "He that saveth his life shall lose it." But if we know that the church exists for the world, we know also that we find our life only by responding to Christ's call from the needs of the world, learning to be present with him where he is at work in the world, by word and deed interpreting for the world the Lordship of Christ within the events of our time.

QUESTIONS

1. What is the meaning of 'neighbourhood' today?
2. Are there 'responsible risks' that the church must take if it is to be the instrument of God in the world?
3. Should Christians work only as individuals in the secular struggles or should Christian congregations enter such struggles witnessing to God's redeeming work?
4. What is the relation between creation and redemption and between the work of the church and of public agencies?
5. How can the church show forth God's mission to overcome the separations, divisions and hostilities that are the sign of our fallen life?
6. Does God ever call the church to obedience by events outside her life, or does change always move from within out?

3

THE SECULAR SETTING OF MISSION TODAY

We have spoken of the need for developing ministries of the laity within the public arenas of contemporary life. We have recognized that the development of forms of church witness in those unfamiliar areas confronts us with difficult problems: one of them being that our experience with forms of association in the voluntary world of residence does not provide us with models in the 'purposive' and 'neutral' arenas of public life. A second difficulty is that a major revolution seems to have occurred in the character of public life—often referred to as *secularization*[1] —and theologians are involved in tortured wrestling with the implications of the change.

A complex of inter-related themes has emerged in the troubling of the theological waters resulting from this struggle with the angel of secularization. Typical phrases pointing to the themes include: "the world come of age," "the secularity of the gospel," "Christianity is against religion," "true transcendence is not a separate life 'out there,'

---

[1] See the article "An Interpretation of Secularisation," in "Towards Structures For The Church in The World," *Bulletin* of the Division of Studies, Vol. IX, No. 2, Autumn 1963. In this Chapter no attempt is made to tackle the whole vast subject. All that is done is to look at some aspects of it which have thrust themselves into the present study.

but a life 'for others.' " The debate centering around Bishop J. A. T. Robinson's *Honest To God* has brought this whole complex of themes to the public eye, and the unexpected crescendo of public response is an indication that it has touched a nest of awakening questions in the public consciousness that are beginning to clamour for answers. Included in Robinson's attempt to speak a relevant word pointing to the proper interpretation of the Christian faith to this secular age of ours, are some major theological and philosophical proposals which have understandably given rise to excited debate amongst the professionals. But our concern here is to dig underneath the debate and search for some of the events that lie beneath the surface. What is happening in our world that is causing these vast shifts in ways of thinking and acting? What are the 'signs of the times'? What is God doing in these changes, and what do they mean for the way we are called to participate in the mission of God?

THE NEW SECULAR HOPE

The first fact of importance is the incredible emergence of man's sense of growing control over the world of nature; a remarkable growth in man's feeling of confidence in relation to the forces that surround his life in this world, and a surging feeling of hope in man's capacity to provide for all men a life of meaningful participation in the free world made possible by the creative mastery of man over nature. In the past the few could so participate, but the masses were condemned to live without real participation in the material benefits of this life; but now this rapid expansion of human possibility is engendering new attitudes, transforming man's feeling about existence, and making obsolete—not without violent social and emotional transitional conflict—vast systems of social organization and religious formulation and practice.

Take for example, the caste systems and patterns of segregation that have marked all our societies till now. In past cultures there seemed to be an irremovable inevitability about them. Human creativity could provide a real measure of secular freedom only for the few; and so social ideologies (and with them religious ideologies) maintained systems of caste and segregated exclusion of groups marked by colour or nationality or class, as a means for justifying the exclusive possession by the few of the means for a life of significant freedom. But now the vast upsurge of human control over the forces of nature is smashing these religious and social ideologies of exclusion, and is giving rise to a seemingly endless series of revolutionary explosions—the revolution against colonialism, the revolution against racialism, and revolutions against all forms of paternalism and oppression.

It is in these phenomena that we feel something of the powerful undercurrents eddying beneath the turbulent waters of discussion concerning the 'world come of age' and the 'end of religion.' The revolution on behalf of the secular is in this connection interpreted as a revolution *for* the participation of all men in a truly human existence in this world. For that reason it is also a revolution *against* all religious and social ideologies which seek to impose predetermined limits to human participation in the fruits of the natural world of creation. And in the judgment of those who are speaking like Bishop Robinson, God is in this revolution, at last making possible free participation for all in a meaningful human existence now. In their judgment too we must now bring to light emphases in the gospel of Christ that until now have been largely hidden. So we speak of "the secularity of the Gospel" with Christ taking this present world so seriously that he became one of us and came to bring the world to maturity in him; of Christianity as being against 'religion' as a separate realm of ideology and of spiritual life which tends to draw men away from participation in the life of Christ as he works to transform the communities of the world; of the life offered by Christ as a life not of other-worldly transcendence, but of the true this-worldly transcendence of Christ as the One whose life is fully "for others."

It is not difficult to see why these themes are considered so urgent. It is because the secular revolution is seen as the work of God bringing us closer to the fulfillment of his purpose for creation. For example, it is assumed that the 'secular conversion' of which we spoke in the last chapter in reference to the transformation of the outlook of the masses in Latin America from despair to hope, is the work of God. It is God who is awakening men to the desire to participate in the new possibilities for a truly human existence offered by modern scientific technological society. It is God who is leading men to batter against the walls of hostility that have divided white from coloured, European from Asian, privileged from underprivileged. These are seen as 'signs of the times,' in which God is calling us to see the presence of Christ at work in the world offering the *possibility* of a fuller participation in the life of his New Humanity.

Of course the emphasis in this last sentence must be on "possibility." When we speak of these 'secular conversions' we must not imagine that we can make a tensionless translation of this occurrence into the language of redemption. In other words, we must not be tempted into thinking that we can see in these historical events the direct fulfillment of Christ's redeeming purpose. In this secularized eschatology we can see the signs of the Goal being offered in the events of history. We can see the possibility here of fuller participation in the life of the New Humanity—the life in Christ in which there is neither Greek nor Jew, bond nor free, barbarian nor Scythian, male nor female. But we can see too the possibility of an even more de-humanized life coming after these revolutions.

THE CALL TO DECISION

For that reason we must be careful to see the way in which Christ is present in the events of world history. And of this we can be sure—he is here as the humble Christ. In offering new life through these events, he offers it as a call to decision. And as always, when Christ offers freedom there is the possibility of the demonic misuse of freedom. Thus at the point where oppressed peoples emerge into the new day of freedom, they can also be newly enslaved by its demonic misuse.

Here we see our missionary calling. It is precisely because as Christians we see in these events a decision set before mankind—the acceptance of the new possibility as a gift from Christ leading toward the life of the New Humanity, or the grasping of this new possibility without confessing its Lord so that the day of opportunity is turned into a day of demonic loss—that we see the urgency of our call to be witnesses to Christ in the midst of the revolution. Here we see the call of Christ for us to be his witnesses in word and deed at those places where he is bringing into being new possibilities for participation in the life of the New Humanity.

We can argue then, that the incredible emergence of the secular world with all its profound promise of participation in a freer human existence in this present world is now calling forth, in a startling new way, forms of Christian fellowship, witness and service in the turbulent stream of public life. We can argue that this can be expected to change the familiar shapes of Christian congregation by releasing it into the secular forms of modern life. But we must beware of concluding that what we can now begin to expect is the disappearance of *tension between the sacred and the secular,* or the dissolution of *the church as a separate institution* through finding its full meaning by participation in the life of the world. Far from it. The necessity of seeing that we must turn our eyes out to what Christ is doing in the world, forsaking our present tendency to locate Christian presence in the relative isolation of private life and answering Christ's call by joining him at the points where he is bringing forth new possibilities for participation in human existence, does not lead to the dissolution of tension. It leads to a rediscovery of *the points of relevant tension with the world.* By seeking to be the presence of Christ at the points where decisions are made, energies extended and anxieties formed, we will find ourselves at the point where Christ locks forces with the principalities and powers. We will discover ourselves at the place of the Cross where there is revealed the true character of sin as well as the true character of Christ's redeeming love.

Certainly the church looks forward to the time when it will wither away and Christ shall be all in all; but it knows that in this present age it will always need to be available to Christ in the world in such a way that through its separate life, he can point the world to his purpose for all life. Certainly also the church looks to the time when we shall need no separate worship, since in knowing the constant presence of Christ we will pray without ceasing; but in this present age we know the necessity of worship as a sign of Christ's redemptive purpose for all men and for all creation. What we need, therefore, is not the dissolution of the tension between church and world, and between sacred and secular; but the proper identification of the tension, so that the church (and the sacred) is not a separate sphere alienated from Christ's work in the secular world. What we need is the presence of the church in worship, witness, fellowship, and service at those points where Christ is offering new life to men in the secular events of time; a church answering its call to erect signs of Christ's Lordship and purpose for his creation at the points of emerging decision in the life of modern man.[1]

Something of what is involved here can be illustrated by reference to an important contemporary debate over the relation of the church to modern secularism.

MODERN SECULARISM

Recently Dennis Munby published in the form of a reply to T. S. Eliot's famous book *The Idea of a Christian Society*, a book that comes right to the meat of our question: *The Idea of a Secular Society*.[2] T. S. Eliot had deplored the central feature of modern secularism—the assumption that we can have a society with no 'established' norms. Secularism is not only banishing the established church; it is also banishing the assumption that commonly accepted religious values are needed for a stable society. Eliot, writing at the time when World War II was beginning to break out, put forward the argument that only a renewal of Christian culture can rescue our society.

---

[1] Pastor Vinay, founder of the renewal centre 'Agape' in Italy, and now leader of a community in Sicily where the members in giving themselves to the needs of the people they serve, inevitably run into danger at the hands of the Mafia, is, with his community of co-workers, a living illustration of the way in which true servant presence 'for others' is still the way of the Cross. He quietly remarked in a discussion about the life of their community, that it is only those who are ready to die who are truly free to serve the needs of their neighbours. This reveals the true secular meaning of the life that is hid with Christ in God; the meaning of being in but not of the world. It is because they have already died with Christ, that they are truly free 'for others.' Now they can be freed from fear, and therefore free for the neighbour —a gift from Christ.

[2] D. L. Munby, *The Idea of a Secular Society*, Oxford University Press, 1963.

It is my contention that we have today a culture which is mainly negative, but which, so far as it is still positive, is still Christian. I do not think that it can remain negative, because a negative culture has ceased to be efficient in a world where economic and spiritual forces are proving the efficiency of cultures which, even when pagan, are positive; and I believe that the choice before us is between the formation of a new Christian culture, and the acceptance of a pagan one.[1]

T. S. Eliot was arguing, in other words, against the secularism that seeks to establish an 'open' society based upon the rejection of a God "up there"—in the sense of a metaphysical 'Other' who establishes all the rules from outside the game. He does not believe that it is possible to maintain such a "neutral" secularism which refuses to use God as an "explanation"; and refuses to accept the necessity for metaphysically imposed norms. T. S. Eliot believes that such a neutral society simply creates a vacuum; and that we must ultimately see society therefore as a battlefield for the gods. If we do not take it over for Christ, and establish a new Christendom, we will leave it open to the pagan ideologies—Nazism, or communism, or some new pagan world-religion.

Munby argues back. He claims that time is proving Eliot wrong—that the emergence of an 'open,' 'neutral' secular society is proving remarkably flexible; and in fact is proving its viability over static societies with pre-established metaphysical norms—including communism and the last parts of Christendom. We should be glad and rejoice in this, however, according to Munby. Secularization seems to traditionalists to be the banishment of God. And it is the banishment of "the God up there" who establishes changeless norms for society; and introduces them through

---

[1] T. S. Eliot, *The Idea of a Christian Society*, Faber & Faber, p. 13.

natural and revealed law, and through first principles in philosophy and science. In fact secularization has done us a service to destroy these God-principles dropped into history from outside; and maintained as plumb lines hanging from a fixed metaphysical ceiling. By wiping these away, secularism is now freeing us to see that *God's presence is within history*—the beyond comes to us from within in Christ.[1] So God's world is seen as one which is truly free for man; and God is seen in Christ as one who is truly free for man—his transcendence is in his complete freedom 'for others.' By this 'secularist' revolt we are freed from static views of society, and static views of thought; and static views of the church. In fact we must welcome this as Christ's work; it *is* the coming of age, which offers us freedom to be with him in his work in the world.[2]

---

[1] Masao Takenaka, *Laity* No. 16, p. 20, makes essentially the same point:

"We must recognize frankly that the age of metaphysics and ideology have passed. We are entering into the functional period. People are keenly interested in seeing things which happen in the life of the world. I believe the contemporary world is forcing us to consider the Christian gospel in terms of the event which happened concretely in history rather than regard Christianity as an abstract doctrine and normative ethic."

[2] Two further quotations from the *Laity* Bulletin on "The Church And The Secular World" will illustrate the way this thinking is beginning to penetrate the church, and the consequences it carries for the relation of the church to the world.

a) C. A. Coulson (p. 38): "We may no longer define secular in the words of the Shorter Oxford Dictionary, as 'belonging to the world and its affairs as distinct from the Church and religion—chiefly as a negative term with the meaning non-ecclesiastical, non-religious or non-sacred.' As Max Warren puts it, we should rather 'define the word *secular* as being of our own age and in our own world. In other words, we will arrive at a fully Christian understanding of Immanuel—God with us—our secular God.' "

b) Mrs. Birgit Rodhe (pp. 46-47): "To us who are torn . . . between Church and world, and searching for a way to be Christians in both Church and world, there is liberation in the words of those who would rather say: 'The world is your Church' or, with the words of

THE GOD 'UP THERE'

It seems to me that Munby offers us in his book a rather convincing exegesis of the suggestions Bonhoeffer offered concerning the nature of a 'religionless' society, and the process of 'secularization' as the work of God. But this does not mean that we have reached a solution to our troubles by joining the Robinsonized Tillich in abolishing all thought of "a God up there," and by suggesting that an adequate account of transcendence (and therefore of God's judgment over human history) is given by speaking of Christ as the one who lives fully beyond himself as "the man for others." This line is full of possibilities, and with the central intention of Robinson we may agree. This becomes clear in his statement[1] that nearly all English believe in God but most are practically atheists for whom "God is a Being over and above (rather than in and through) what for them makes up 'life.'" They believe in a God who is not involved in the affairs of their daily existence. Robinson is concerned about the extent to which the God pictured in people's minds as 'out there' becomes the focus of a religiosity filled with man's projection of his own desires: a capricious God who answers my private or group wishes— a 'God' not open to the purifying judgment of what God is doing in the world. The God 'out there' can be the one who meets the private needs of the racist; but who does not have to be faced in the midst of the secular revolution

---

John Robinson in *Honest To God,* 'The charter of the Church is to be the servant of the world.' And who will, also with Robinson, use for a definition of the laity the words of Abbé Congar, saying that a layman is one to whom the things of the world are really interesting in themselves, for whom their truth is not as if it were swallowed up and destroyed by a higher reference—for instance by how far they can be turned to the service of the Church or used as occasions for evangelism."

[1] *The Honest To God Debate,* p. 229.

against his cherished social patterns. The God 'out there' leaves his followers too exempt from the fires of judgment in the events of history; he is the God of religion, whose worshippers see their Sabbath religiosity as something apart from what God is doing in the world. They do not comprehend the saying that the Sabbath was made for man, not man for the Sabbath. Because God is 'out there,' the things pertaining to God do not change: God is a religious conservative—he does not have to be watched as one who can be expected to break into the midst of our contemporary life with major demands upon the form of our worldly existence.

In his attack against *this* God 'out there'—a God only too evident, not only among the nominally religious in England who do not take seriously the God in the midst of the events of world history but also among many of the religious in the U.S.A. whose God is also a convenient absentee from all but their private spiritual life—we can see the force and relevance of Robinson's attempt at reformulation.

Similarly we can see the strength of Robinson's attempt to come to terms with what Bonhoeffer meant by a world 'come of age.' Here we face the new feeling toward the world produced by science and technology. With the sense of man's increasing mastery over the world, there has developed the feeling that there is less and less need to 'call in' God as explanation and as a sporadic intruder. Now man thinks of day to day events in terms of inside or worldly forces that he is able to understand for himself. In this sense, therefore, he has 'come of age'; he has grown up and can accept responsibility for his own life to an extent that his old thought world of religious forces 'out there'—God, angels, demons—never dreamed as possible. Now for this reason, Robinson believes that if we keep the "out there" symbols for God, we will think of God as the one who comes in only at the times we need help—in our weakness; at times of crisis such as moral defeat (if there are no adequate human resources available) or death. What we need instead is now to abandon the God who comes in from outside—like the capricious forces of an animistic world-view—and to speak of God as 'the ground of Being' who comes to us in the ordered processes of our scientific world, and in the turbulent events of our world history.

THE NORM OF HISTORY

With the central intention of Robinson's attempted re-statement we can agree. Our concern, however, is with the need to maintain that 'transcendence' which will help us to see God as the one 'outside' in the sense that he brings even our best human intentions under his judgment, and which will help us to discern the presence of Christ in history because we know him as the one who is Lord of history. For unless this transcendence is maintained, our mission will be lost in the tides of history with no guidance beyond the stream to lead us to our destiny.

To illustrate: Robinson speaks with Bonhoeffer of the transcendence of Christ as one who lives 'beyond himself,' 'for others.' Good. But in saying this we are expressing a conviction that there appeared in history *a norm* that is in some sense beyond history. We are saying that Christ appeared in history as one who reveals the goal towards which history is moving. Now in what way does this differ from T. S. Eliot's norms? It would appear that when Eliot says that we must have norms outside the process, he may be justified. Here we are at the heart of the issue. T. S. Eliot's norms are outside history—timeless. But Christ as norm comes to us in history as the one who reveals the goal of history,[1] as the 'beyond' who does not deny the 'open'

---

[1] This links up with the question of *the marks of the church*—the marks of the church are not timeless characteristics of an institution

character of our secular society, and does not distract us from the call to seek God's purpose within the changing streams of worldly life.

We would agree then with T. S. Eliot on the need for norms, and would agree with the traditionalists in their insistence that a normless world is one which is at the

---

immersed in time. They are 'signs' in history which make the church the harbinger of the Goal. This links up too with the question of liturgy. It was often argued that the Catholic Mass was a powerful witness to the Gospel *because* of its timelessness—because of its Latin, unchanged through the centuries—and its timeless vestments, music and movement. But now this is increasingly being recognized as an inadequate witness to the true nature of the Gospel. When the ritual first emerged it played out in Byzantine Court Ritual the drama of Christ as King of Kings. Christ moves into this structured world of the social hierarchy and points forward to his transforming work; for finally all the ranks kneel together from Emperor to slave to share in the one redeemed life of the reconciled family of God. The ritual was designed to show how Christ brings the *present world* within the drama of the Gospel in such a way that we see the firstfruits of our final life in the completed Kingdom. The *timeliness* of the Gospel is what is here displayed; as the rhythms of our contemporary life are taken up into the redeeming rhythm of the shape of Christ's redemptive work.

So now we are having to seek to do for our day in the liturgy what the great liturgy did for the centuries in which it originally emerged. The eucharist is truly celebrated when the rhythms of contemporary life are so taken up into the shape of Christ's redeeming work, that Christ the host gives us the 'foretaste' of the final goal. That is why it is not a true celebration in East Harlem unless there we see Christ breaking through the division between white and Negro and Puerto Rican; cultured and despised; rich and poor; just as he broke through the divisions between Emperor and slave in the Byzantine Ritual. This is why experimental liturgies seeking to take up the rhythms of today's life in music, word, movement, are also beginning to struggle for birth.

In one sense I believe it is true to say that the true shape of church life is first of all liturgical—that is, the shape of the church emerges as we allow the life of our world to be drawn up into the shape of the drama of Christ's redeeming work in history. As the moving present is brought within the "once-for-all" sacrifice of Christ "for others," Christ then writes the shape of our worldly obedience for us, and calls us out to join him in the midst of his continuing reconciling work as he leads us on to the goal that is constantly given to us in the drama of the liturgy.

mercy of pagan ideologies. But we would insist that the true norm is an historical norm given us in Christ. This means that when we are called to act in the midst of contemporary events, we do not turn to abstract, timeless standards. Because Christ is our norm; and because in him is revealed the true nature of the End—a life 'for others'; a New Humanity in which the walls of hostility disappear and we are truly open to each other; a life of the New Creation in which men increasingly share in the full possibilties of God's creation—*we are free to watch for the call of God as it comes to us in the events of history.* Where we see the promise of the dividing walls of hostility being broken down; where we see the promise of widening participation in the open community of the New Humanity; where we see the drive towards the opening of the creative possibilities of life to those formerly excluded; there we see the presence of Christ working out his purpose; and the call of Christ for the presence of his followers. We are to read the 'signs of the times'; we are to ask for the gifts of the Spirit which will enable us to discern the presence of God in the events of history and will enable us to be witnesses who by word and deed seek to bring the world to a recognition of its living Lord.

A THEOLOGY OF PARTICIPATION

These norms, given to us in the events of the life of Christ, are not static norms. By their very nature they reveal their meaning to us only as we are participants in the continuing events of history. That is why they call for a 'pilgrim theology' that speaks out of the living dialogue between the Bible and the world. And that is why there is a growing feeling that a radical change is required in theological education—both to bring the learning process into closer touch with the missionary participation of the church in the life of the world, and to bring the training of the ministry of word and sacraments into relation with the training of the laity for their ministries in the secular world.[1]

---

[1] If 'coming of age' means the readiness to take off the swaddling clothes of fixed norms; the removal of the scaffolding of 'Christendom' and the 'establishment' and the deliverance of the Christian fellowship into an 'open' world where witness to Christ has to be given through a 'style of life' in which ultimate meaning is disclosed in the midst of the struggle for free participation by all men in the life of the New Humanity, we must expect a radical change in the place of parsons in society. Munby refers to this (op. cit., p. 65):

"In past ages, there has been some justification for regarding the clergy as representative of all men. Today such a claim would be ludicrous." In other words, the norm setting function of the clergy has been dissolved. They no longer fix the rules as the representatives of the 'given' norms—even to the point of 'just prices' and 'moral absolutes.' They no longer represent in their life the 'ideal' which can be expected to produce (with understandable flaws!) the pattern toward which the community could aspire. Instead the norm-setting function of the church is passing to the laity in their ministries in the secular world, as they learn to exercise their servant ministry 'for others' in the midst of the struggles of the world's life.

Munby believes that there is urgent need for an understanding and acceptance of this changed position of the parson. He quotes with approval these words by T. R. Morton of the Iona Community (op. cit., p. 87):

"The minister has become the greatest obstacle to the development of the congregation into responsible adult life. . . It is taken for granted that the minister should be the arbiter of the congregations thoughts and life. . . . Today in the absence of any effective teaching on vocation the only thing that the member can do is to take the minister as his model. . . Where he can follow the minister is in those parts of life which are common to both—the personal, domestic sides of life. So this private side of life is seen as the one plane in which the Christian life is lived."

There are two points needing to be made here:

1. In the classical Protestant tradition the focus of the norm-setting role of the clergy has been in their commission to preach the gospel, administer the sacraments, and tend the flock. They were the guardians of the community's faith and life. This necessity for 'delivering' the faith still exists; so presumably in this sense the representative role of the clergy still exists.

The fact, then, that the norm given us in Christ is one whose meaning as disclosed to us in the midst of history, drives us into a dialogue of word and action with our fellow human beings. It reminds us that it is only as we seek the way of obedient life in Christ that the unfolding character of that life becomes apparent. Christ is the sign of the 'historical' nature of our norm; the Holy Spirit is the sign that Christ becomes known to us as Lord as we participate with Christ in his servant life in the events of our time.

NATURAL LAW

We can illustrate this truth by reference to the debate over natural law as it relates to the field of ethics. It has been the claim of some that unless there are accepted ethical standards for common action in the struggle for an orderly society, we can only expect chaos. The problem is, however, that these supposedly permanent standards fail to reveal themselves in common form to people of different religious and ideological persuasions. But perhaps this is the clue to the dilemma. On the one hand, "natural law" proponents have pointed out that words such as justice, order, peace, freedom, are words that have common usage across the ideological conflicts. On the other side, opponents have quickly pointed out that only the words are

---

2. The new factor is that with the 'coming of age' of the church, the clergy are no longer able to carry in themselves the responsibility for the way the Word and Sacraments must disclose their meaning and life within the currents of daily affairs. Now the clergy must be delivered into the midst of the world's life through dialogue with the laity at the places where the total ministry of the Body must reveal its servant character. The clergy in the past were partially outside the stream of time—handing down the norms by which life in time was to be governed. Now they are being freed into the stream of time and into unity with the laity in the one mission and ministry in the world. There, in the world, the people of God must gather and serve; and there in the midst of their mission the Holy Spirit brings the understanding of the living word of Christ.

common and that the contents given them by the different ideologies are in severe conflict. How can both affirmations be true? The reason would seem to be that the words disclose the common problems of human existence; the *common questions* that men are forced to face; but that the words themselves are neutral—empty vessels waiting to be filled.

For example, justice describes a common human question—a universal problem. "What is the right way to reconcile the conflicting claims of individuals and groups?" There is no universal answer; and thus in the struggle for justice in a particular situation such as the race revolution, different groups can be participating in the struggle—each attempting to fill the word with the content of their own faith. Moslems, humanists, racists, Christians, all recognize the problem; but the real question is: "Which group will win the battle to fill the word with content?"[1]

T. S. Eliot was not wrong then when he pointed to the need to fill the norm words with Christian content. Where we must take issue with him, is in the way this content is supplied. He argued for the view that the Christian faith supplies permanent fixed norms; and that an institutional and theological 'establishment' is a Christian aim. We would argue that the Christian faith draws us out into a common endeavour with our fellow-human beings in the struggle for true participation in human existence. We would say that the words such as justice, peace, order, freedom, indicate the common human questions, and that as Christians we must be engaged in the struggles of human society to fill these words with the presence of Christ. We can participate in a common dialogue and often in common

---

[1] See p. 83f below for an illustration of the importance of this. Here we see a central aspect of the secular mission of the church—the mission by deed and word of seeking to fill the norm words and the behaviour patterns that operate in the public worlds with the content of the gospel.

action with those of other philosophies and religions, because with them we share the same questions and the same struggle to answer the questions in life. But our task, in word and deed, is to tell them of Christ who truly poses the questions and who alone can fill their questions with true meaning.

Our task then, in this dialogue and common action, is one of hard struggle against the false content given these questions by the philosophies and religions—a false content that at times becomes demonic, and leads the Christian in this dialogue to witness 'under the Cross.' But our struggle too must be in the name and spirit of the humble King who fought the battle not by worldly methods that oppress opponents, but by servant methods that seek to overcome them by the way of love.

The true content these common questions receive from Christ is not an abstract timeless norm. It is a timely meaning that is disclosed as we seek as Christians to participate in the struggles for justice and freedom, for peace and truth, as those who witness to Christ as the Living Lord who enables us to be free for each other because he gives us the true freedom of justified sinners. We witness to the One who out of the midst of this servant life discloses the true character of justice, freedom, peace, and order.

If this is so, it has a great deal to say to us concerning the forms of Christian life and witness. Again it reminds us that there is no timeless place for Christian congregational life. It reminds us that true congregational life is that which is seeking to be the disclosing presence of Christ's Lordship in the world, participating with others at the points of the struggles for justice, freedom, peace, and order, and seeking to be the servant community in whose life the true decisions of life are clarified, and in whose fellowship the gracious reconciling presence of Christ is declared as the 'firstfruits' of the Kingdom of God.

QUESTIONS

1. What is the nature of the "world" God loved so much that he sent his Son?
2. What is "secularization"?
3. In offering new life, what is the nature of Christ's call to decision?
4. Is Christ calling us to join him at the points where he is bringing forth new possibilities for participation in human existence? Identify some of these.
5. How is God's presence discerned in history?
6. What is the meaning of 'pilgrim theology'?
7. What does it mean to participate with Christ in his servant life in the events of our time?

4

PARABLES OF MISSIONARY OBEDIENCE

HOW IN THE WORLD?

On a good many occasions since writing *Where In The World?* the question has been asked: "All right, we are convinced that the church must turn its life out into the world; that we must find new structures of missionary obedience. Now tell us: when are you going to write *How In The World?*." It's a natural question. And yet we must be careful how we seek to answer. When Jesus was asked 'how' questions it would seem that he refused to answer them directly. Thus when the lawyer asked the question "Who is my neighbour?" he was really asking a how question. Jesus had taught "Love your neighbour," and now the lawyer wanted the 'how' spelled out. The scribes had: by drawing circles of responsibility. Love has one meaning in the circle of the family, then in the circle of the nation, and to the stranger when he moves inside these circles. But when it comes to the Samaritans—the Jews have no dealings with them. And so the lawyer wanted Jesus to spell out his statement by telling how we are supposed to translate love of neighbour into practice. But Jesus didn't answer directly; instead he told a parable.

And this parable response was a regular practice. By these stories and sayings Jesus sought to train the eye and the ear to see and to hear those calls of need from the world that asked for immediate response. He did not provide techniques or methods as such; for these tend to dull the need for sensitive decision in changing circumstances. In his stories and sayings, and in his own deeds, he gave a living outline of life in God's Kingdom; and sought to train his disciples to respond in such a way that their life as believers and as a community should witness to the life of the Kingdom of which they were already citizens and to which they were moving.

We must, therefore, resist the temptation to try to write a blueprint for the emerging structure of church life. In a major sense structures will take care of themselves. Just as in architecture we often hear the saying 'form follows function,' so in the life of the church it is true that structure follows obedience, and the primary need is the recognition of the types of obedience which are now required of us.

THE PROBLEM OF OBEDIENCE

At this point, one cannot escape the feeling that our questions of 'how' are all too often excuses for not undertaking an obedience which we sense will prove too costly. Paul Kraemer, the Dutch sociologist, speaks of the troubling questions that arise as we ponder "the present state of the churches in modern urban—industrial society."

> Why is it . . . that the intensive re-exploration of the Bible in the light of today's completely changed circumstances has yielded such a rich harvest of new and inspiring theological insights, but that notwithstanding this the churches as a whole appear to be in a very deep rut, indeed? For years we have been told, over and again, that the Church *is* mission, that the true

Christian mission is to serve the world, to show soli-
darity with all men. . . Yet, the constant harping on
this theme of an open and 'other-directed' Christianity
has, thus far, not resulted in any real breakout of the
introverted, 'tradition-directedness' of established
Christendom. At the most, mention can be made of
a few scattered 'experiments.' . . .

One cannot help being struck by a couple of nasty
thoughts . . . First, . . . Just as their ancient predeces-
sors, the medicine-men or *shamans* in primitive religion,
the theologians and clerical leaders of our day seem to
have a strong belief in the magical force of sheer verbal
repetition . . . Second, . . . one truly doubts whether
many leading churchmen do not flinch instinctively at
the tricky consequence involved in their brave new
theories, when it comes to the point of putting these
theories into practice. . .

If there is to be a real renewal of the Church, there
is no escape from tackling, in a most thorough way, the
'problem of forms.' It is not enough to re-think the
being of the Church in our contemporary situation in its
theological implications; it also is necessary to come
to grips with the sociological implications. The new
wine of ecclesiological concepts springing from a seri-
ous confrontation of the biblical message with the entirely novel conditions of present day society cannot
be put into the old bottles of an institutional framework which developed with the needs of men in ages
past.[1]

We come back then to the sociological and religious
captivity of the churches.[2] It would be senseless to refuse
to acknowledge the powerful vested interest against
change: material, because of the vast institutional invest-
ment in the forms of past obedience; emotional, with the

---

[1] *Concept V,* September 1963, p. 27-28.

[2] See footnote on p. 36 in Chapter II.

great reluctance to leave the world of the familiar; professional, with the fear of leaving the forms of church life for which we were trained, to venture out like Abraham into the unknown. The strength of this natural conservatism poses real problems of strategy for would-be reformers. Is it necessary to leave the institutional power in the hands of the conservatives, and to concentrate attention in the areas where the authorities are prepared to give freedom for new ways—in the inner cities where even the most conservative must confess the failure of the traditional; in industrial settings where the church has found no effective entrance; in the face of crisis needs where the servant presence is obviously required? Or is there the possibility of a breakthrough at administrative levels, with those in authority feeling sufficiently free to seek to devise a strategy for the forms of church presence in the world which are now demanded by the 'signs' of what God is doing in the events around us?[1]

I suspect that the answer is that we must keep working at both ends. Wherever there is freedom for new obedience we must seek to occupy the room that is given. In other words, as well as looking for signs in the world, telling us what God is doing and where we must join him in his work, we must also look for signs in the church showing us where God is giving us room for obedience—opportunity for bringing together the form of the church and the need of the world.[2]

---

[1] See the article by Letty Russell in *Concept VI*, January 1964, "Reflections on the Yale Consultation."

[2] This can be put another way. On the one side we need careful Biblical and theological study on the question of how we are called to seek the signs of God's presence in the world. At the same time we must watch what is happening on the moving edge of the church's relation to the world to see what God may be teaching us out of the struggle for contemporary obedience in the world.

PARABLES

In what follows we seek to give 'parables' of what God is doing to open the church to the way of missionary obedience. They are chosen in the hope that through them God will open our 'eyes' and 'ears' so that we will learn how to recognize the shape of obedience to which we are being called in our situations.

a) CRISIS RESPONSES

i) Lifeline[1]

In March 1963, the Central Methodist Mission in Sydney, Australia, where Alan Walker is the minister, opened an institute whose sole purpose is to be available to need. Alan Walker announced to Sydneyites that help is as near as a telephone. In a city where need never sleeps, so also the presence of the church's witness to the love and mercy of Christ should be unsleeping. A team of volunteer specialists—social workers, lawyers, doctors—is available, and as the couriers of immediate help "trouble teams" in radio cars answer the cries emerging from the complex world of contemporary need. Hundreds of calls come in each week; and the attempt is made to answer each need in the form in which it arises—witnessing to Christ's redeeming love by presence, by deed and interpreting word.

Here it is important to notice that the external structure —building, radio-equipped cars, staff—followed in the wake of response to need. Sensitivity to the call of Christ from the world of need has led to the response in which the church takes shape around the recognized need. Form (structure) then followed function.

---

[1] See report in *Time,* January 24, 1964.

ii) The Voices of Need

Alan Walker's way of servant approach to the needs was that of announced availability; the offer of readiness to serve the needs at whatever time they emerge. In Taiwan a group of Christians decided to go in search of those needs. In the Report of Section III of the Mexico City meeting of the Commission on World Mission and Evangelism, it was affirmed that:

> We are called:
> a) constantly to ask where God is at work in the world.
> b) to take the incarnation seriously: to be "Christ to our neighbour" (Luther), by serving and suffering through involvement in the arenas of the world's struggles not only as individuals but as old and new forms of congregations.
> c) by word and deed to interpret for the world the Saviourhood as well as the Lordship of Christ in the events of our time.

In illustration the Report then went on to give an example:

> Thus we see the significance of Christians from a city church in Taiwan going out into the police stations, trade unions, government offices, and finding that "in these encounters they discover a shape of Christian obedience being written for them by what God is doing in the structures of the city's life outside the church."[1]

b) TO MAN IN HIS STRENGTH

We could multiply examples of response to crisis—a drug addict's clinic in New York; a legal clinic to help Puerto

---

[1] In Fleming and Wright, pp. 78-81, there is an account of the work in Industrial Evangelism undertaken by the Presbyterians in Taiwan, of which this is part. It is a most instructive report.

Ricans in the same city; communities of identification with the dispossessed in New Haven, Connecticut; or in Sicily with Pastor Vinay. These are evidences of eyes and ears trained to see and hear the call of Christ from the altar of human need. They are evidence too of hearts strengthened to respond in costly identification.

But Bonhoeffer reminded us that it is not enough for us to come to man in his weakness. Our society is marked by increasing self-confidence in man's mastery over his world; and we face the question whether we can witness to Christ as Lord at the points of modern man's strength and self-confidence. This need is calling out an increasing response.

i) Crossroads Club

Alan Walker draws together on a weekday at noon, a representative group of decision-makers from the life of Sydney. His aim is to meet them at the point of their strength and concerns—in their secular integrity. The subjects under discussion are the key issues emerging in the life of Sydney. The dialogue with the gospel to discover the concrete meaning of the Lordship of Christ is thus initiated from the events that are occurring and in which these men have responsibility. If it is discovered that out of that dialogue there arises a call to missionary action, there is freedom to move from the point of dialogue to the appropriate forms of action.

ii) Mission to Industry—Japan[1]

In many parts of the world attempts are being made to penetrate the lost world ('lost' to the church; but often anything but 'lost' in their own self-awareness) of industrial man. Sheffield Industrial Mission in England; in Germany the work of men such as von Bismarck in the Ruhr; in India the team ministry in Bangalore based on the Church

---

[1] Quoted from Fleming and Wright, pp. 76-78.

of South India's Cathedral Church of St. Mark; in the U.S.A. in the Detroit Industrial Mission. Here we take an example from Japan.

In the Kansai area, the chief industrial belt of Japan covering the three great cities of Osaka, Kobe and Kyoto, a group of churchmen, including students, ministers, and laymen have been striving for the last eight years to present the Gospel of reconciliation in terms relevant to the life of the industrial worker, and in relation to the industrial structures. One of the men who has been associated with this experiment from the beginning writes of it as follows:

We first started with the training of four theological students as interns. After the end of the intern experiences, two of them indicated that they would like to devote their lives to this frontier ministry. There was no budget available in the existing evangelism programme. So we started to raise money by ourselves to support two full-time industrial pastors. As the result of five years of experiment, we now have four full-time workers in this flexible ministry in industrial society—two pastors, one young woman, and one missionary, working as a team in this new group ministry. There are four basic points which we are keeping in mind in this 'frontier experiment':
(i) to find out where laymen are in industrial society within a concrete social context, to encourage them to form occupational and professional groups, and to help them to fulfill 'the work of the ministry' in the concrete world of labour;
(ii) as workers who are not tied up with a particular congregation, to be more flexible and sufficiently mobile to make a thorough and deep contact with the leaders of various organisations in industrial society, gaining their confidence and holding a real dialogue with them;
(iii) to help the churches in the region to become a

witnessing community in relating their life to mission, their worship to daily work, and their fellowship to witness;

(iv) to explore the ecumenical dimension among Christians of different backgrounds working in a common task and in the same field of labour.

(Masao Takenaka in *Christ's Ministry—And Ours*, p. 30.)

An important experiment has been the setting up of Labour Schools, lasting from four to six months, and intended to be long-term education-processes to provide ordinary workers with the right kind of labour education. This work is supported with a monthly publication 'The Worker,' which in 1962 had 8,000 paid subscribers, and deals with the problems of industrial society in a way that makes it acceptable to non-Christian workers also.

At the level of the theological seminaries, special courses and seminars on Christian responsibility in industrial society have been instituted, and courses in social ethics related to industrial society have also been begun. There is also a 'Student in Industry Programme' under the National Christian Council, whereby about fifteen students each year share in ordinary industrial jobs for a month in the Osaka area, spending the evenings in discussion of problems, and hearing expert lectures on industry. This has meant that there are now ministers coming into the Church with a genuine understanding of the problems of industrial society. In all these and in other ways, the Church in Japan is finding a greater flexibility and openness to society, and is helped to respond more faithfully to the needs of a particular situation.

iii) Ceylon—To Past and Future[1]

One of the places of assumed strength in much of Asia and

---

[1] Op cit., p. 83-84.

Africa is at the point of the great religious and cultural traditions of Hinduism, Buddhism, Islam. In Ceylon the Christian Ashrams seek the way of identification with the Buddhists at the point of their strength, so that on *their* ground the dialogue may be opened in which Christ may witness to himself as Lord.

> The Christian Ashrams, which are centres of devotion and meditation, whose communal life is based on the traditional patterns of Sinhalese Buddhist piety, are open to all who will come in, and are in fact the focus of a real dialogue between the Church and the resurgent self-conscious Buddhism of the island. Using indigenous forms of worship, and living in a simple rhythm of prayer, study and manual labour, these Ashrams succeed in "remaining close to the heart of the nation's life and culture, while engaged in a living dialogue with other great religions, and proclaiming the Christian message of the Cross."

The other side of the feeling of strength in Asia is in the emergence of the new industrial society, and in Colombo the Christian Worker's Fellowship (CWF) is seeking to move out into this new world.

> The CWF of Ceylon is affecting the structure of Christian congregations in two ways: First, it forms Christian cells within trade unions, political parties, and work groups, but it makes very clear that these cells must not become pressure groups, which could be suspected of trying to be communal efforts to influence these organisations. Thus, no actual decisions are made at such cell meetings; there is only full discussion of the issues in the light of the Gospel. Secondly, the CWF attempts to show the relevance of worship and liturgy as part of the total life of the worker. The special service which is held every May Day—which is significantly held early in the morning so that the workers can later join in other May Day celebrations of Unions

and Parties, the Christian workers first form a procession with the red flag, followed by working implements during which they chant a workers' litany in indigenous Sinhalese forms. Arriving at the Church, they enter bearing the flag and tools right up to the altar where they are laid, and remain throughout the liturgical service and Communion. Thereafter, they are again taken out into the world. Many have borne witness to having received a new understanding of the place of worship within the Church's missionary task, as a result of this lovely and indigenous service which is, incidentally, entirely planned and written by laymen.

c) RESPONSIBLE PLANNING—
   SAN FERNANDO VALLEY

The examples so far have been of particular approaches to a group, a problem, a religion; and many others could have been chosen—ministries to artists, to political decision-makers, to leisure-time.[1] But one aspect of need has not been mentioned—the need to undertake responsible planning for the whole segment of a modern city and for seeking to develop ministries to public worlds, and the interrelation of these with the ministry to man in his residential world.[2] What makes this difficult is not just our lack of experience in knowing the true nature of these worlds to which we must witness, but also the fact that unless the approach is ecumenical, it is doomed to futility. The worlds of public life—such as mass-communication, leisure, urban planning, social welfare—have a secular unity which makes absurd the attempt to approach them denominationally.

---

[1] This last is an area of increasing importance. Those wishing to know something of the rapid expansion of concern here may write to the Department of Leisure-Recreation, National Council of Churches, 475 Riverside Drive, New York, New York 10027.

[2] See *Where In The World?*, pp. 110-112.

And with all our brave words at ecumenical meetings, it is still extraordinarily difficult for churches to free themselves sufficiently from their separate ways to undertake common planning and action in a sizable city segment.

One such possibility is now in the planning stage. It is mentioned here in the hope that before long it will move from planning into operation, and in the belief that even if this should not occur the fault will be with resistances in the present life of our churches, not with the plan itself.

In the San Fernando Valley area of Los Angeles, the Lutheran Church of America launched an exploratory project in 1962, with Pastor Clifton Weihe as its Director. Its purpose is to discover the shapes of public life in the Valley, to train laymen in the understanding of their Christian missionary task within these worlds, and to seek to relate these ministries in the public arenas to the work of the present local congregations. The Lutherans saw this from the beginning as requiring ecumenical cooperation, and undertook their task in this spirit. In 1963 Miss Marlies Cremer, the German sociologist from the Evangelical Academy at Bad Boll spent considerable time in the area investigating the structures of these public worlds: mapping the patterns of decision making, the structured forms of need, the inter-relation of public and private worlds. From her work grew the suggestion that the time had arrived for developing an ecumenical team-ministry which would work with the churches in the area from the heart of Los Angeles out into the Valley in developing a responsible strategy of mission in the whole area.

Out of discussions with Departments of Evangelism, the suggestion grew that this project should be an international one. Miss Cremer expressed the view that here in the Valley was a remarkably "pure" example of the emerging shape of secular society—relatively free from the institutional life of the past, and throbbing with the inter-related structures of the technological age. Here was a place where Africans, Asians, and others, could see the future shape of their societies. Here was a place for responsible experiment in ministries to these new forms. As a result, the possibility of making this a Joint Action for Mission Project (JAM)[1] was discussed with the World Council officers, and the plan now is for an international team to undertake this experiment in ministries to public life, in cooperation with the churches of the area.

The significance of this plan is not just the projected experiment. Its significance lies also in the attempt to work through the ecumenical and denominational bureaucracies to bring the plan into operation. If it should come to fruition, those who are close to despair with the institution and are inclining to the belief that renewal can come only from outside, may be given a new lease on institutional hope.

d) FACE TO FACE GROUPS:
FORMS OF PARTICULAR PRESENCE

With the emergence of our complicated urbanized world, the tendency is for man's roles to be de-humanized. This makes it increasingly essential that the church should seek small group forms of presence with man at those places where he is seeking for identity. In this way the church can witness to the concern of Christ for each person; and it can help the individual discover the meaning that God gives to his life within the particular roles he plays in the changing shape of contemporary life.

---

[1] The Division of World Mission and Evangelism was authorized by the Third Assembly of the W.C.C. at New Delhi, to develop projects in which the churches would share their resources in major problem areas of mission, in the belief that the way to unity must follow the path of 'responsible risk' in the field of experimental action as well as the path of theological discussion in the area of Faith and Order. The DWME is in the process of seeking to develop at least one such project on each continent.

'House-church' developments in various parts of the world, for example, may be pointing the way to a revision of the form of the residential congregation as it seeks to change its role from that of being the centre of Christian participation in all of life, to that of bringing the presence of Christ to man in the world of the family and the particular needs of the residence community. Other examples are leisure-time ministries; small cells working with particular groups in business or politics; or attempts such as the truck-stop ministry on the Kobe Road near Tokyo to serve the needs of those whose humanity is being squeezed out by the demands of our mechanized society.[1]

e) RESPONSE TO GOD'S ACTION IN THE EVENTS OF OUR TIME

The church is called to seek the guidance of the Spirit in reading the signs of the times, in order that she may learn what God is doing in the events of the times in such a way that she may witness to him as the Lord of history through word, deed and fellowship.

The great difficulty in understanding what God is doing in history should not tempt us into withdrawal from this witnessing task. Instead it should remind us of the need to search for the marks of God's presence in the world, and of the need to learn how to listen to what God is saying to us now as the meaning of his revelation given once-for-all in history comes to life for us as the Risen Christ comes to us now by the roadside and calls for us to witness to him as the Lord of history.

A CASE STUDY—"THE FREEDOM MOVEMENT"

The North American Working Group has taken the relation of the churches to the race revolution as a case study in

---

[1] See the W.C.C. Monthly Newsletter on Evangelism, March 1964.

the question of the missionary structure of the church. Have the churches helped or hindered the fulfillment of the mission of God in this struggle? What is happening in the "Freedom Movement"—can we see the signs of the work of Christ in the midst of it? What can we learn from this concerning structures for contemporary mission? The Working Group held a special meeting on the subject in February 1964. A panel of people who are deeply involved in the Movement—Arthur Thomas (NCCC Commission on Religion and Race), Andrew Young (Southern Christian Leadership Conference), Sandra Hayden (Student Non-Violent Coordinating Committee) gave statements, and were cross-questioned at length. Small groups carried on the discussion and reported back to the plenary group, and further discussion wrestled with the issues that emerged. What follows is my attempt to state the significance of this Case Study for the Missionary Structure discussion.

1. "The Movement" or "The Freedom Movement" is a general term including the variety of action groups involved in the struggle for the rights of Negroes and other minority groups in such areas as Civil Rights, Housing, Employment, Education, Access to Public Facilities. "The Movement" is largely of an *ad hoc* character in which Negroes have found themselves drawn into the midst of a revolution, inspired by the brute facts of an existence in which they are continuingly excluded from the rising levels of secular hope in the world around them.

2. The nature of the revolution is such that many Negroes find themselves consciously seeking to translate their Christian faith and commitment into the struggle—both in the definition of the goals to be sought and the methods to be employed in moving towards the goal. They find themselves joining in the struggle with those who are non-Christians. Here what was said in Chapter III about

terms such as justice, freedom, rights, dignity, as neutral words pointing to common human questions—but words which are empty vessels waiting to be filled[1]—is given concrete illustration. And here we can see the vital importance of the missionary task of struggling to fill these words with Christian meaning.

In this struggle, Christians have gained many of the key leadership positions, and have helped in giving these words real Christian content. We see this in the vision of the goal that inspires much of the Movement, a goal of an open community of love, with the human dignity of all men being recognized regardless of race. In the way it is given expression it is clearly inspired by the vision of the New Humanity in Christ.[2] We see the Christian content even more clearly in the methods being promoted for movement towards the goal—the non-violent method of forgiving love, looking to the winning of 'the enemy' as a brother, in the knowledge that each cannot be free without the other. In allegiance to these goals and methods, Christians are able to work together with non-Christians, for they must meet on the common secular ground of ethical language; but the missionary task at this point is that in the dialogue as to the meaning of action these secular words

---

[1] By 'empty vessels' it is not implied that non-Christian groups have no content in the use of these words, or that Christians have a monopoly on true content. As Bonhoeffer discovered (*'Ethics,'* p. 177), we often find men from unexpected sources fighting for what we know in Christ to be the true content of justice and freedom. What is meant by 'empty vessels' is simply that these words do not carry their own content, and that in the midst of the ideological struggle to fill them with conflicting meanings, we have a missionary task of witnessing to the content Christ gives them.

[2] Compare the rejection of Black Muslim goals, and of any talk of separate communal groups with the rights of one pitted against the other.

are filled with the content of the Christian faith—they are taken captive to their true Lord.

3. In the Movement, many Negro Christians work under the keen sense that they are being obedient to a call from God that has come to them out of the midst of the revolution. Andrew Young spoke of a sense of destiny—of a belief that God is using the Negro in the South as a sign of hope: a sign that through the gospel of Christ He can break through the tragic barriers of race conflict and open the way to truer human community. He spoke of an inchoate sense of awareness that often breaks through in their prayers—a feeling that God has delivered them as his children into the costly centre of this crucial battle to break through the demonic racial and class limitations by the creative power of forgiving love. He spoke of their self-identification with the stories of Israel; of their awareness that without the shedding of blood there is no remission of sins; of their feeling that God is calling them to be a redemptive suffering group for all the people of America.

Here then is a people (not all; or even most; but a faithful remnant) who see their participation in the events of history as shaped by the redeeming purpose of God in Christ.

Are these people here in the midst of the struggle the sign of the true people of God—the true congregation?

4. In this struggle, those with this Christian consciousness work with many who are not consciously Christian. But what of the common shape of their lives that begins to appear? Do we see in their common lives the evidence of the presence of Christ?

a) We see in their lives a common quality of commitment—a life of self-abandonment 'for others.' In itself, of course, this is no sign of the true presence of Christ. Men oftentimes sacrifice their lives for the demonic. "Though I give my body to be burned. . . ."

b) But here the 'for others' is seen in the struggle for the inclusive community, and the giving of themselves to seek the opportunity for a truly human life for all.

c) Here too *the way* used is often the way of love, so that we see here the suffering servant shape—even though in great imperfection.

d) We see here thoroughly mixed motivations—people joining the Movement for the wrong reasons, and many whose lives are deeply distorted. But here too we see people whose commitment is far better than their lives, and who by living toward their commitment are often purified as by fire—a new being emerging slowly in the midst of suffering. Is this a living symbol of justification by faith—sinners whose lives are stretched out beyond their sin to a living hope and who by this commitment are being sanctified—saved by hope; gradually becoming what they already are in their commitment; often failing, but constantly rising again from failure to move on towards the goal of their high calling?

Do we see here then, out of this mixed community, the work of Christ as he sustains the community of action by the central commitment of believers, and in the process works to bring the latent church into open being through the common struggle 'for others'?

5. In the midst of this mixed community 'the marks of the church' would seem to be present—even though their fullness may not be manifest. Thus in the Monday night meetings, preparing for action, there is often powerful preaching: the Word brought into touch with the concrete issues before them. The Biblical drama is heavily used: here is a call for total commitment, a readiness to give one's life in the cause of true community. Here too there are prayers: and prayers in which the living needs of the situation of action are brought within the circle of God's redeeming work in Christ. Word and worship are brought

into living contact with the day to day questions arising in the battle to change the structures of the world toward the Goal of true community.[1] The problems of life are taken up into the gospel, and orders are given for the direction of their action in the world.

The question this poses for our present congregations is whether they are wrongly situated in relation to the emergence of questions arising in the world that demand decision. Is the Word then being truly preached? Or is there a famine of the Word in our local congregations because it is not in living contact with the situations of required obedience?

The tension in the Negro churches between this "worldly" form of Christian community in the Movement, and the Sunday congregations in their separate residential world, is of real importance. Andrew Young asked whether the movement from Sunday to Monday was not in fact a stumbling back and forth between the 18th and 20th centuries. He asked whether the two forms of the church can be brought into truer unity. This clearly affects the question of the relation of the sacraments and ministry to the 'church in the world.' The ministry which has emerged in the world community of action, for example, is 'charismatic.' Leaders are chosen by the gifts they reveal in the midst of the Movement; not by their institutional place in the church or community. Again this poses the question as to whether the church as it commits itself to action in the midst of events will not find itself returning more to charismatic leadership.

6. It is noticeable that in the Monday night meetings the

---

[1] Hence the name "The Movement": they see themselves as *in via,* just as the people of the New Testament called themselves the followers of "The Way"; for they were moving out with Christ towards the End.

forms that are used are the forms of the old revival meeting with which the Negro has long been familiar. The preaching, with audience participation and personal testimony; the symbolic commitment through prayers and songs which draw forth the total response of the self within the group; the stress on the free movement of the Spirit—all these are old. But what has happened here is the turning of these out into the world, so that the emotion is not directed inward. The direction of attention is to what ought to be happening in the world and the way it should happen. God is calling us to obedience at the place of his action. He is calling for active witness by word and deed to his Lordship as it is being made known in the events of the world.

Does not this indicate the basic freedom of the church in the use of structures? In the New Testament we have the sense of a variety of forms: is the crucial factor the *direction* of life and not the *forms* used to train us for that direction? Are structures less important than direction?

7. So far we have spoken of what is happening in the revolution, and how the Christians are participating at that point. We must now ask how the traditional churches are responding. By and large the answer must be confessed as massive failure. There are important regional differences—largely reflecting the different concentrations of Negroes; but also influenced by different traditions. But traditional congregational structures have not responded well to the call of the situation in the light of the gospel. While the South has responded much more negatively, in the North as well the dominant mood has been to avoid any response that would cause institutional discomfort, or threaten a schism. In the South most white congregations have acted either by inaction—strongly effective exclusion of discussion—or when challenged to action, by the rejection of the forces calling for change—even to the ousting of ministers,

and hostility against 'outsiders' who have challenged them to reconsider their ethos of segregation.

When challenged, the common response has been: "Yes, we should do more; but we can't. We are so dominated by feelings of prejudice amongst our members that to push any harder would result in a split." And so opposition to action in the light of the gospel is justified by the need for institutional self-preservation. One Bishop put it: "Isn't the church worth saving?"—thereby identifying the church with the present segregated congregations. Is it true of such churches, in fact, that "he that saveth his life shall lose it?" Will the church only participate in the fruits of salvation when it is willing to risk its safety in the service of the world, and in witness to the crucified Christ?

There are, of course, some positive responses in the churches—commissions on religion and race; participation in the action by many ministers and laity; but most of the official response has been on the level beyond the congregation. It would appear to be true that the local residence congregation is so much a prisoner of the segregated community to which it is related, so much a captive to the segregated patterns of exclusive life against which the revolution is directed, that within that structure there is very little freedom for the gospel.

This poses a very key question for the churches: Since it has only been by breaking outside the structures of congregational life that the church has gained enough freedom to witness to Christ by word and deed in the midst of the revolution, what does this suggest in terms of necessary change in the structure of congregational life?

Sandra Hayden (SNCC) told of her youthful commitment to the church, but of her reluctant decision to leave it. "I felt I had to choose between being in the church or being in the world struggle . . . I don't see people finding in the church the resources they need to overcome the fear of race. It is not preparing them to act to change the things that are wrong in the world. So I have found a community in the Freedom Movement." As a group, she confessed, its quality was mediocre. "But we all know we have a job to do together." And so she is working in a voter registration project in Mississippi—giving her highly-educated life at a point of real risk, for no visible return; for the freedom of others.

The first thing this seems to demand is that we must develop ways of breaking out of the isolation of congregations within segregated community lines—not just race; but class, culture, income, ethnic group. The church is called to be the 'firstfruits' of the new creation; a revelation of the way in which Christ is breaking through the dividing walls of hostility between race and race, culture and culture, class and class, nation and nation, and is making of the two one new man. Is not a congregation isolated inside a race, class, culture ghetto a 'heretical structure'?[1]

---

[1] See *Where In The World?*, pp. 82 ff. Werner Simpfendörfer has provided some comments on the term which carry a needed warning against its too-easy use:

"1) Heresies arise (according to Karl Barth) through 'the arbitrary selection of subsidiary themes out of the whole revelation, thus missing the Christological centre and turning a subsidiary theme into the main theme.'

"According to this, structures are heretical:

"a) If they obscure or deny what the 'Christological centre' signifies for the Church and for the world—God's gracious will towards the world and towards human history.

"b) If 'subsidiary themes' are turned into the main theme, so that biological, sociological, historical or other phenomena are given the status of the main theme.

"2) Nevertheless, the concept of 'heretical structures' remains problematical.

"a) First of all, I Corinthians 14 must be considered in relation to church-structure. 'God is judge.' On no account must one (or several) forms or structures be regarded as 'heretical,' if 'multiformity' is the aim. Apparently, here lies a danger of morphological neo-fundamentalism.

A further suggestion is that churches can only maintain their calling to be the 'firstfruits' of the new creation, revealing the power of Christ to bring forth the New Humanity, when their life is turned out in response to what God is doing in the world. She must be ready to take shape around the changing forms of need and to participate in the work of overcoming the demonic powers that constant-

---

"b) On the other hand the 'procedure of diagnosis' against 'heretical structures' presupposes a *potestas ordinis (juris dictionis?)*. This power is invested in the whole Church. Any decision as to what structure is to be regarded as heretical at any time can, therefore, be taken only by the Church as a whole—through dialogue and consensus.

"c) Not only have heresies turned *partial* truths into absolutes. Heresies have also arisen through emphasising *neglected* truths. Most heresies have therefore always announced essential truths. The same should apply to 'heretical structures.' They should not simply be eliminated. One should rather recognise the truth in such structures, and then *'allocate them to their right place within the whole.'*

"3) 'Heretical structures' can be diagnosed as such only if there exists a corresponding *'orthodoxia'* or a 'confession' with 'the right structures.' As long as such formulations are not available, it is impossible to condemn any existing structures.

"Furthermore it should be possible to define more precisely the conditions under which heresy becomes truth and truth becomes heresy. For one can hardly overlook the fact that 'the Christological centre' can (and must) be expressed quite differently in different sociological and historical circumstances. And this also applies to structure."

Here we may discover the real clue to the renewal of our present congregations. By recognizing their present isolation within racial, class, cultural, income boundaries; and by confessing that the church is called to be the firstfruits of the New Creation in which the power of Christ to break through these barriers is revealed; congregations could open themselves to creative strategies of renewal:

linked parishes across racial, class, culture lines;

church school programs which would provide continuous inter-racial, inter-cultural experience, and train the children in the need for work in the community at these points;

planned participation in community organizations in order to give to the world a vision of true urban renewal, working for open communities of shared responsibility;

This concern stresses the vital need to escape from congregational isolation, and to accept planning responsibility at area levels—both denominationally and ecumenically.

ly threaten the health of the human community. The real failure of congregational life is here revealed as introversion—care for itself; with the abject failure to care 'for others.'

ANOTHER TEST CASE:
THE PRAGUE PEACE CONFERENCE

It should not be imagined, however, that events around us normally will bear such clear resemblance to the familiar marks of Christian presence as the Freedom Movement. Here the direct influence of Christian tradition is great; but the problem is much more difficult in a case such as the Prague Peace Conference. There, Christians in Czechoslovakia and other "Iron Curtain" countries have called upon Christians from across the world to join with them in a movement for peace. Some from the West, like German Bishop Otto Dibelius, have condemned the movement as a demonic attempt by the Communist world to draw Christians into their cold war struggle by weakening Western determination to resist communism. From the East, Czech theologian Hromadka has answered that communism has much in it the Christians must resist; but that nevertheless we must see in it also God's judgment on our Western failure to live by our Christian faith. And in the peace movement he sees the secular hand of God, calling Christians to confess their failure to witness to the Prince of Peace and to join together in the struggle for peace in such a way that we can witness with Hromadka to the One who alone is our peace.

In this vital struggle between Christians (and non-Christians), we see the great difficulty of reading the signs of God's presence. Hromadka has Biblical texts to which he can appeal. If Cyrus was God's anointed; Assyria the rod of God's anger—then we should be prepared to ask whether communism is not similarly God's judgment on our Western way of life. If communists use 'peace' as a cold war slogan, is not its appeal as a slogan due to the failure of a so-called Christian world to seek peace and pursue it? But similarly has not Dibelius Biblical support? Does not the devil disguise himself as an angel of light; and is there not here evidence of demonic misuse by the communists of the legitimate aspirations of men for peace, while all the time they are seeking to use a peace-front movement as a weapon of ideological warfare?

The difficulty then of reading the signs of God's presence can be sensed. But must we not also see the tragedy of refusing to be involved because of this difficulty. If it is true that the communists are seeking to use the peace movement as a front for ideological warfare, is it not possible that this very fact constitutes a call from God for the church's presence in the midst of this struggle—witnessing to Christ as the true peace who alone can fulfill the aspirations of mankind? If it is possible that Hromadka is innocently being used by communists in the cold war; is it not also possible that Bishop Dibelius is on the other side an innocent captive of the Western cold war, and that the church is called to be present at this point of conflict witnessing to the One who offers to break down the dividing walls of hostility and bring true peace out of the mdist of enmity?

Enough has been said, perhaps, to suggest the urgency of struggling with the questions of the marks of God's presence in the events of our time, and the importance of discovering ways of being present with Christ in the midst of these events. At this point we have much to learn in terms of the forms of missionary presence to which we are being called.

THE SHAPE OF THINGS TO COME

In the parables of Jesus taken together, we are given a sense of the whole shape of the Kingdom of God. Are there, as yet, sufficient 'parables' to give us today some sense of the emerging shape of the church for our time? In one sense the question requires a negative answer; for in one sense what we are learning is that we must not look for a fixed shape, but for a mobile church free to respond to the movement of God in the events of our time. Nevertheless, there are characteristics of these various responses which may be important in guiding us into the future.

After reviewing what they see happening in Asia, Fleming and Wright conclude:

> It is possible that in all this we are on the verge of a real 'breakthrough' from 'religion' to a 'secular Christianity' which, while understanding the nature of the Church as a people called into being and sustained by God, yet insists that both the gathered life of that people in worship, and its scattered life in the world, must be truly 'in and for' the world, and for the 'outsider' and his whole culture.

Then they go on to ask whether we have beyond that any more definite outline of the forms of our community obedience. They conclude:

> What the actual structures will be, we cannot dare to say. These *must* emerge from the *obedience* of a church convinced that it has a mission to the world, from a *venturing faith* that understands the Holy Spirit's guidance not as a dogmatic proposition, but as a reality of every-day life and decisions, and from a *conviction* that, somehow or other, the Church must be embodied in structures that are related to the world's structures, or there will be no meeting with men at all, no encounter, no proclamation, no mission. Because new structures will emerge from this kind of situation, we cannot dare to be dogmatic about the forms and structures the Church's life will take.
>
> But we can see certain shapes looming up, as it

were, out of the mist. From the experiments going on
in Asia, which we have interpreted as signs both of
judgment and renewal, we can discern something of
the shape of things to come.

It is the point of view of this study, that these experiments or signs of renewal are not just parallel and
supplementary to the 'normal' working of the churches,
but are ventures of faith that call in question the
'normal,' and compel the 'ordinary parish congregation'
and the 'ordinary parish priest or pastor' to scrutinise,
carefully and prayerfully, the shape of church life
as it is, for the sake of the church life that might be,
given a church that means business in today's world.

In this task of scrutiny the present congregations are not
left without guidelines as to the forms of present obedience.

Though the actual structures in most cases have still
to emerge, we can see something of the shape of these
emerging structures. . .

By this phrase, we mean patterns of church life that
will encourage and foster a real Christian penetration
in all the places of human life, where men live, work,
make decisions, and 'are men.'

'Place' should be understood not just in terms of residential communities and 'parish system,' but in terms
of the complex of communities that make up modern
life in Asia today. . .

To achieve such structures will mean taking seriously
the complex nature of society in Asia today, its changing nature, its centres of power and decisions, its associations and groupings, and so structuring the Church
that Christians can be involved responsibly in these
'natural' groupings as part of a Church that is 'living
for others' . . .

Another aspect of 'structures of Christian presence'
taking shape in and around the structures, shapes and
concerns of the secular community, is that in this way,
Christians can be truly open to the problems of *all men*

in that part of society. This means an openness to 'structures of joint concern, enquiry or search' as between Christians and non-Christians. . .

Still another aspect and result of such 'structures of Christian presence' will be *true indigenisation*. . .

It will come only as congregations, sure of their mission, and orientated towards life in the world, try to make their faith, witness and life 'at home' in the various areas of contemporary Asian culture, structuring their life within and around the natural communities of men. They will not appear as people who know all the answers. They will appear as people who have a tremendous trust in Jesus Christ, and the Holy Spirit, to lead men into truth that is not just religious truth for church people, but is God's truth for the Market, the Stock Exchange, the Labour Union and the Board of Management.

ALL IN EACH PLACE

The Report of Section V of the Montreal Conference on Faith and Order in 1963, included this statement:

Searching questions are raised as to whether the institutional patterns of our local churches and denominations are not increasingly obsolescent, in the light of our deepened understanding of the nature of the unity we seek, and because of the impact of secular challenges to our common calling. . .

They spoke of the ecumenical recognition of the fact that we are called 'all in each place' to witness together to Christ, and of the recognition that 'place' must refer not only to local neighbourhood, but also to the public worlds, and also to "wider geographic areas such as states, provinces, or nations, and certainly refers to all Christian people in each place regardless of race and class."

The Report was concerned with the need for "local church" to be understood in such a way that it refers to all the people of God in their locality in the full sense. It refers specifically to divisions which deny this missionary calling:

We are shamefully divided by racial prejudice and discrimination. This denies the dignity of man, subverts our unity in Christ, and stultifies the mission of the Church. God is judging our racially divided Christian communities through the contemporary revolutionary events in many parts of the world. In Christ there is no defence or excuse for the wilful continuation of groups, church meetings or fellowships which are racially exclusive. We therefore call upon Christians in their local churches to show the marks of Christian discipleship whatever the cost.

We are also divided by ethnic, cultural, and tribal loyalties. We recognize that, in the providence of God, human life is sustained by communities of language, custom, and culture. The churches have properly ministered to their people in and through their varieties of tongues, customs, and art forms. Indeed cultural unities have sometimes nourished Christian unity. But these divisions of the human family too often mask our oneness in Christ, and are maintained with a passion that makes them idols. The ethnic, cultural, and tribal divisions between and within congregations in each place call all Christians to self-examination and repentance.

The Christian community is often divided by rigid denominationalism. While we rejoice that there are some signs of co-operation for the witness to the unity of the Church in some areas, in many places churches with common confessions of faith still remain denominationally separated, long after any defence of such separation can be made in the light of the gospel. Institutional self-interest often maintains division in local churches to the detriment of the mission of the Church. The churches are called to overcome inertia and denominational pride, which alienate believer from believer and hinder the proclamation of oneness in Christ.

Identification with a particular social class; preferences for a particular style of life; commitment to a political philosophy or party; achievement in economic life and education, etc.—these also often threaten the wholeness of the Christian community in each place. In themselves, these factors represent a social diversity which often serves human good. Yet the same loyalties must not be allowed to supplant the loyalty of a congregation to its one Lord.

Christians are today being brought together by the mobility of people, by migration, by nation-building, by the struggle for human freedom and justice and even by the social and political oppression of the Church. Christians (both as individuals and as a body) are often passive recipients rather than active participants in the processes which can enhance human and Christian community. With opportunities such as these which are made possible by God, there is also given a command to form local Christian communities that witness visibly to our oneness in creation and redemption.

Unity is the fruit of Christian discipleship, and the latter takes various forms. A common protest against unjust laws which create or enforce racial divisions will make clearer the oneness in Christ. Crossing social barriers for Bible study and prayer, for labour and recreation, can bring new forms and levels of unity into existence. Co-operative activities of ministry and fellowship, when done even in advance of consensus within a denomination or of the strict interpretation of canon law, can promote unity. Mutual visitation and personal contact can break new ground. Participation in the worship of God through unfamiliar cultural idioms, and expressions may lead to new experiences of all being one in a given place.

If the unity which is "God's will and his gift to his

Church" is to be made visible, it is essential that local churches accept the missionary obligation which God has given to his whole Church. More insistently and urgently than for centuries, we are being asked: "Are you really sharing the life that is in Jesus Christ, because to share in it is to take part in his mission to the world?"

This Report makes one thing clear. We may often feel like Abraham—as though we are asked to go out not knowing where we are going—but our real situation is more like that of Jeremiah—we want to resist the clear word we have heard. Already there is so much light on the way of our obedience, that if we are prepared to start acting on the basis of the way we know we must follow, we can go forward in the confidence that Christ will give us the further light we need as we proceed.

Our basic problem is not light; it is obedience.

QUESTIONS

1. How can we "in our church" train our eyes and ears to see and hear those calls from the world that ask for immediate response?

2. Can it truly be said that our church leaders today "have a strong belief in the magical force of sheer verbal repetition"?

3. Do we find in our church a "powerful vested interest against change"?

4. What signs in the church do you see where God is giving us opportunity for bringing together the structures of the church and the needs of the world?

5. How can our church minister to man in his strength and self-confident mastery—as well as in his weakness?

6. Is there need for groups of Christians who engage in "full discussion of the issues" that relate to their work life "in the light of the Gospel"?

7. Is God calling the church through the racial struggle to be in fact what it really is in commitment? How is our church responding to his call?

8. In what respect is our unity or our disunity a sign of our obedience or disobedience?

CONCLUSION

A SERMON   THE ALTAR IN THE WORLD

Matthew 5:23-24: If, when you bring your gift to the altar, you remember that your brother has anything against you, leave your gift before the altar, and go, first be reconciled to your brother and then come and offer your gift.

We sometimes speak of the hard sayings of our Lord; and surely this must qualify as one of the hardest. We come to the altar only because we are in need; we come because we hope the promise of God is true, that "he that cometh unto me, I will in no wise cast out." But here when we come with outstretched hands, Jesus seems to repel our approach—and with harsh words that apparently deny the claim that we can come in confidence knowing that he is more ready to forgive than we are to ask for forgiveness. Here he stops us short: "Put your gift down. Now think: Is there anybody in the world who has anything against you? If so, leave your gift, first go and be reconciled with your brother."

Perhaps your first reaction is that this is not too harsh— not too unreasonable. "I'll mend my fences quickly and soon be back." But what is it that Jesus teaches us that our brother can hold against us?

1. He teaches us, first, that our brother can hold against us any sin of commission: any unkind word or deed by which we have damaged the fabric of human fellowship. In the words immediately preceding our text, Jesus re-

minds his hearers of the commandment against murder, and draws out the ultimate significance that lies beneath it. Behind the commandment against murder lies God's intention that the human family should live in unbroken fellowship; therefore anything which damages that fabric of fellowship comes under his judgment. If you so much as allow the words 'you fool' to creep to your lips, you are sinning against your brother; and must seek reconciliation.

So if, when you come to church bringing your gift to the altar, you remember anyone in the world who can hold against you any unkind word or cutting comment, or selfish act—any way you have damaged fellowship—go back into the world, and first be reconciled to your brother.

If we allow our minds to move out across the wide network of our human relationships, we may well be excused for asking: Will I ever get back? Is Jesus making worship in church impossible? Is he on the side of those reckless ones who seek to abolish 'religion' and desire only to drive us out to the unsupported task of doing good—when I myself am not good.

But Jesus takes the case against us much further.

2. He teaches us, second, that our brother in the world can hold against us our sins of omission—the opportunities we have had to help one in need, which we have failed to accept. Remember the Parable of the Good Samaritan. How many times have I passed a brother in need, failing to help where it was in my power to go to him? Remember too that Jesus speaks of the two who passed by as religious men—a priest and Levite—reminding us of the danger that the very *fact* of religious routine can so lock its faithful followers within the boundaries of institutional procedure, that they are no longer free for human need: no longer free to respond to God's call from the world.

So if you come to church bearing your gift, and remember that the needs of religious performance and the demands for keeping the institutional machinery running, are such that the life of God's people is no longer free to meet the needs that are passed by on the road of life, put down your gift there before the altar, and go, first be reconciled to your brother.

And now the question becomes more insistent. Will we ever get back? Has Jesus too joined those who cry—'suburban captivity'? But who will meet our needs—our religious needs?

Or take the Parable of Dives and Lazarus. The rich man dining sumptuously at his table, and the poor man at his gate—starving, racked with disease. The rich man's sin was that he failed to see the need: his eyes unwilling to see the need to which his heart was unready to respond. When Albert Schweitzer read this parable one day, it suddenly came to him that he (with his brothers in Europe —and the U.S.A.) was the rich man dining sumptuously, and at his doors were the millions of beggars in Africa and Asia. He left his gift there before the altar, and went to be reconciled to his neighbour in Africa. He has not come back. He went out into the world to meet his neighbour's need.

But still this is not the full case that Jesus makes against us.

3. He teaches us, third, that our brother can hold against us the sins he has committed against us for which we have failed to seek reconciliation. "For if you do not forgive men their trespasses, neither will your Father in heaven forgive you your trespasses."

Something of the depth of this teaching is being uncovered for us by some of the Negro preachers such as Martin Luther King, Jr., in the midst of the Freedom Struggle. In their Monday night rallies this message rings out: "Brothers, you are going out into the world to claim your freedom now, as true children of God. As you go out to claim your birthright and look your white brother in the eye, you will be tempted to hate. You will know he has sinned against you. He has robbed you of your dignity. He has ground you under the heel of injustice. He has locked you up in housing ghettos. He has stolen your right to full education and fair employment. He has excluded you from open participation in the life of the community. You see him as a sinner, and are tempted to hate. But . . . Brothers, you are going out into the world as servants of Christ. Your white brother can hold against you his need of forgiveness. He is a guilty man; and in the name of Christ who forgives us all, you must help to make him free."

So, if you bring your gift to the altar, expecting to receive forgiveness, and remember that your brother in the world needs your forgiveness, put down your gift, first be reconciled to your brother. "For if you do not forgive men their trespasses, neither will your Father in heaven forgive you your trespasses."

Go out into the world. But will we never get back? Is Jesus here making worship in the sanctuary impossible? In one sense, yes. It *is* his aim to make sanctuary worship—isolated from the world—impossible. Jesus freed worship from its isolation—freed it for the world. "Destroy this temple. . . . " Jeremiah had witnessed to the terrible temptation to locate faith in a place of separation, so that it was not free for the world; a temptation that besets the 'religious' people most of all—"You who cry the Temple, the Temple, the Temple of the Lord." Now Jesus brought that judgment to completion. He destroyed the worship of the separated sanctuary; but now in its place he put the living temple of his Body—now free *in* the world. And the Church is the Body of Christ; the people of God gathered around Christ's moving presence *in* the world.

If when you bring your gift to the altar . . . Does this

make worship impossible. No; it defines it. When we come to the altar, we come and meet the Christ who is there to drive us out into the world—to meet him there. When we come, we come that we may have our eyes made sensitive to the needs of the brother at our gate, our ears made open to the cries of the brother by the roadside. We come that we may meet Jesus Christ and be trained to read 'the signs of the times' calling for our servant presence in the world of human affairs.

But what about our needs? Are they forgotten?

In Matthew 25 we read the Parable of the Great Surprise. Judgment Day is pictured; but of course it is the present structure of our lives that is under review. What do they disclose? A life that is truly a 'sign' of the Kingdom of God; or a life that is false—a living lie? In which of the two groups do we belong—sheep or goats?

The key to the surprise lies in the words "When I was hungry, you gave me food; when thirsty, you gave me drink; when I was a stranger you took me into your home; when naked you clothed me; when I was ill you came to my help; when in prison you visited me."

The key? You gave *me* food. Christ's words may seem harsh when he drives us from the altar made with hands; but here is a gracious word of promise. Christ is ready to receive our gift on the altar of human need. You did it unto me.

Here is Christ's call to the church. Your institutional life is sick; sick with self-concern. Leave your gift before the altar. You will find your life by taking shape around the moving shapes of human need. There you will find me; the gracious one; the forgiving one; the redeeming one. To the church it must be said

"He that saveth his life shall lose it; but he that loseth his life for my sake and the gospel's, will find it."

PB 4655-2
4
H-4

PB 163-3